More Parables from the Back Side

More Parables from the Back Side

J. ELLSWORTH KALAS

Abingdon Press
NASHVILLE

MORE PARABLES FROM THE BACK SIDE

This book is printed on acid-free paper.

Library of Congress Cataloging-in-Publication Data

Kalas, J. Ellsworth, 1923-
More parables from the back side / J. Ellsworth Kalas.
p. cm.
ISBN 0-687-74041-X (binding: adhesive : perfect : alk. paper)
1. Jesus Christ—Parables—Sermons. 2. Methodist Church—Sermons. 3. Sermons, American—20th century. I. Title.

BT375 3.K35 2005
226.8'06—dc22

2004018337

ISBN 978-0-687-74041-3

08 09 10 11 12 13 14—10 9 8 7 6 5 4 3 2

MANUFACTURED IN THE UNITED STATES OF AMERICA

To my dozens and dozens and dozens of cousins
at Tabernacle Camp Meeting
who first welcomed me as their preacher in 1964
and so many times since then
that I've come to think I belong to
the remarkable Taylor family

CONTENTS

INTRODUCTION

In the early 1990s, Abingdon Press published my book *Parables from the Back Side.* To my surprise, and no doubt to the surprise of the publisher, people are still buying and reading this little book as we move steadily into the twenty-first century.

In one sense this continuing popularity shouldn't be a surprise. I speak not of the quality of the book I wrote; I know better than that. I'm thinking of the fact that the subject of my book, the parables of Jesus, have fascinated people for some twenty centuries, ever since our Lord first spoke them to people in the villages and on the roads and in the countryside of Galilee and Judea. And here's the astonishing fact: These stories speak as powerfully as ever in what some call our postmodern world. They still comfort the seeking, challenge the learned, and trouble the arrogant.

For several years, kind readers have asked, "Why don't you write ***More*** *Parables from the Back Side*?" I have finally decided to do so—not only because of these gracious urgings, but because the parables themselves have pressed me. The parables keep saying to me, *Look at me again; what do you see?*

So I have looked again, and yet again, and this book is part of what I've seen. I pray that the chapters that follow will not only bless your understanding of the parables, but that they will cause you to fall in love anew with the Bible and its wonderful, unceasing claim on our lives.

—J. Ellsworth Kalas

CHAPTER 1

The Value of the House

MATTHEW 7:24-27: Everyone then who hears these words of mine and acts on them will be like a wise man who built his house on rock. The rain fell, the floods came, and the winds blew and beat on that house, but it did not fall, because it had been founded on rock. And everyone who hears these words of mine and does not act on them will be like a foolish man who built his house on sand. The rain fell, and the floods came, and the winds blew and beat against that house, and it fell—and great was its fall!

A generation ago a television personality used to close his show by saying, "I'll see you again tomorrow, the Lord willing, and if the creek don't rise." I thought it was just a cute, colloquial saying until I lived for two years in the Kentucky mountains. There I discovered that the saying might be colloquial, but it comes from common sense based on experience. Kentucky has more miles of creek and river beds than any state except Alaska. In a matter of minutes, a hard rain can turn a lazy creek into a thundering wall of destruction. Roughly once a year the news media report a tragic story of someone who, driving home during a rainstorm, ventures across a familiar bridge, certain the water is manageable, only to be swept down the creek to death. A few days later, riding over the same creek, you can't imagine there could ever be danger in such a pretty little stream.

I suspect just such a creek bed could have been in view when Jesus told his story to a gathered crowd. In that part of the world such places are known as *wadis*—watercourses that are dry except in periods of substantial rainfall. I can imagine a boy looking at his father as Jesus tells the story, then shifting his feet uneasily as he looks at the wadi on which they're standing.

Like so many of Jesus' parables, the one in Matthew 7:24-27 is a very simple story. This is part of the wonder of the parables: The stories are so deceptively simple that one might rush through them without thinking, or one might say impatiently, "Of course! Everyone knows that." But there's the rub. If we don't "know" the message well enough to conduct our lives accordingly, then we don't *really* "know" it.

Jesus had just finished an extended period of teaching as he led into this parable. The response to his teaching was probably as it often is when someone challenges us with ideas that call us to change. No doubt the people were cautious about buying in with the teacher from Nazareth. His insights were intriguing, but it was clear that he was outside the establishment. Still more unsettling, his teaching was more demanding than that of the conventional rabbis. So at this moment when his listeners were weighing the message, Jesus threw down the gauntlet. Some people, Jesus said, would hear what he had said and would act upon it, while others would hear and do nothing. Jesus described these contrasting responses with strong language. The people who would act on his teachings were wise, while the others were foolish.

There's no genteel tentativeness here, no talk of "now we all have a right to our own point of view." Jesus may acknowledge that you have a right to your point of view, but he makes clear that your point of view may be wise or it may be foolish. Contrary to a currently popular sentiment, all points of view don't have the same value. Nor does Jesus commend the foolish ones for being "sincere" about what they believe, because sincerity doesn't help much when one is terribly wrong. Nor does Jesus suggest that there are multiple ways of looking at these matters; quite simply, there is a wise way and a foolish way, and that's it.

Some matters are like that, you know. The biggest issues of life are not like choosing between the several brands of cereal at the supermarket, nor even like choosing between several different colleges. The biggest issues of life are so vast in their reach and their consequences that those who choose rightly are wise, and those who are wrong are fools. This is hard language; but since we have only one life with which to cast our vote, someone had better spell out the matter clearly.

So Jesus resorts to a story that is just as clear as the identifying language he has chosen to use. Two men are building their homes. From what Jesus tells us, the homes are comparable in every way except one. Both, apparently, are well built. Both men care about the kind of house they build, because they're going to live there. The only difference is this: one house is built on rock and the other on sand. A city boy like me might not notice this difference. I know more about literature than I do about gravel and concrete, so if I were buying the house, I could be fooled.

But not the people to whom Jesus is talking. These are people who know land and property. They know where to build and where to avoid. If they choose a bad location, it isn't for lack of knowledge, but for some lapse of judgment. Rightly, then, Jesus describes these people as foolish. They have not erred for a shortage of information, but because of a deliberate choice. When Jesus says they are people who have "heard," we see them as informed and therefore equipped to "build"; but for some peculiar reason, the choice of the man who decides to build his house on sand contradicts reason and the very data of their lives. Please keep this clearly in mind: The difference between these two men is not a difference of ability, of knowledge, or of opportunity; it is a difference of choice. The one chooses wisely, the other foolishly.

At first there's no evidence of wisdom or foolishness. As I indicated a moment ago, both men are building good houses. As you walk through the area, you might admire them equally. But one day there's a storm. This is the surest thing I can tell you about this parable. In life, you can count on it that one day, somehow, some way, somewhere, there will be a storm. In a world where sickness exists, where accidents happen, where marriages are broken, where friendships are betrayed, and where the changing economy means jobs or businesses lost, everyone is compelled at some time to deal with a storm. Some people, Lord have mercy, live with storms most of their lives; my heart aches when I think of some such that I have known. Some seem to escape the storms for a long time; in such instances they often are particularly devastated when at last the storm comes their way. When I was a pastor, I was astonished by those persons who responded to the storm by complaining, "Why should this happen to *me*?" I found it hard not to reply, "Why should you be exempt? Didn't you know that to live on this planet is to meet a storm now and then?"

But let me confess that at times the storms can catch any of us unawares. The sun shines so pleasantly on life that you think nothing of it when there's a nagging pain. But when the doctor says the pain is an advanced malignancy, suddenly we find ourselves swept by a storm. I knew a man who returned from work one day to find a note from his wife that she had left and would not return. He told me he had no idea such a rupture was coming. Perhaps the sunshine of his career had made him insensitive to the storm that was shaping up in his marriage. All of us are sometimes caught unawares by one kind of storm or another.

Well, it's when the storm comes that you find out something about your house. As Jesus tells the story, the whole issue is in the foundation. One man had built on rock, the other on sand. You wonder how this could be. Anyone should know better than to build on sand. That's the point Jesus tries to make. This is a parable for those who have some knowledge. They know what house-building is all about. Why would such a person deliberately choose to build on sand?

In some instances, I think it's because the person has the "it couldn't happen to me" outlook. I remember a military officer from World War II who said, "If you tell a group of ten soldiers, 'Nine of you won't come back from this assignment,' most of the group will say to themselves, 'I sure feel bad about those other fellows.'" We know, statistically, that a certain percentage of persons who start out as social drinkers will become alcoholics. "Somebody else," the woman says. Some of life's conducts are like Russian roulette; you ought to know when you begin them that there's a chance you're playing with a loaded pistol. But most of us are optimists enough that we think we're among those who will beat the odds.

Other people build on sand because, frankly, the land is cheap. They're the folks who always look for a marginal deal. They cut their ethical decisions at such a close line that sometimes they end up on the unethical side. They justify with the oldest of excuses: "Everybody does it." Obviously, *everybody* doesn't do it; perhaps too many do, but not everybody. Besides, morality isn't established by a plebiscite; morality cuts more deeply into life than a majority vote. Those who look for a shortcut to happiness are easily persuaded to buy sandy property. They know they want to get that dream house as fast as they can, and they can get it so much faster if they don't have to invest so much in the land.

Then there are those who are taken with life's externals. They're more interested in the things that impress their neighbors and friends than in foundations. "It's much easier to sell cute bathroom fixtures," a realtor tells me, "than to sell the pipes that deliver the water to the bathroom." I regret to say that when some people put their lives together, they spend more of their time, their money, and their character seeking to impress other people than in choosing a good foundation. I suspect that if there were some kind of plastic surgery for the soul that could be done in a simple, even if fairly costly, operation, the church would get a lot of takers. Being born again may happen in moments, but there are no sudden saints. The sequel to being born again is that we're supposed to grow up (isn't that the purpose of being born?), and that's a long process.

I think, too, of a line from Sir James Barrie's play *The Twelve-Pound Look*. "One's religion," a character says, "is whatever he is most interested in, and yours is Success." Some people are, indeed, so taken with success, with money, with public recognition, or with the accumulation of tangible and intangible benefits that they don't pay a great deal of attention to life's foundations.

So, one way or another, for one reason or another, some people choose to build their house on sand. That's what bothered Jesus. He had finished another session of teaching, and implicit in each of his lessons was a call to follow. Jesus could see that not everyone was going to follow. As a matter of fact, a great many would not, and only a few would. And Jesus said that those who heard the truth and didn't act on it were fools.

Why such a hard word? What is the measure of the decision that cuts the line so sharply that those on one side are called wise, while those on the other are called foolish?

Just this: *the value of the house*. The reason the foundation—or the land on which the men in the parable were building—was such an issue was because of the value of the structure that was going to be built on that land. If the man had been building a chicken coop, we could forgive him for choosing a questionable foundation; a small coop doesn't cost much, and it doesn't take too long to build. But a house? That's quite another matter.

Especially when you get only one house. Most of us charge into life as if we were going to be able to develop a whole subdivision of lives, so that if this one didn't work out, we'd move into another just down the street. But life isn't like that. We're given just one, so we'd better build it on a foundation worthy of the house.

Take, for instance, that part of our house that we call the body. It is a magnificently engineered entity, this body of yours and mine; and it is remarkably resilient. We can feed it so many wrong things, offer it sleep at careless intervals, and ignore so many of its warnings, yet it recovers in quite miraculous fashion. That is, we can make all sorts of bad choices regarding our bodies and still survive. This is especially true in these days of modern medicine and skilled physicians. But eventually the stuff we put into the foundation of living—the choices we make—will put the whole house in danger.

So, too, with the still more wonderful part of the house that we call the mind. I'm a novice with the computer, but I know enough to marvel at its intricate capacities. Then I pause and think of the human brain and remind myself that I carry on my shoulders a computer that can never be duplicated. But I can mess it up. I can invest my mind in idleness, on the one hand, or in frenetic ambition, on the other; I can feed my mind on pornography, on resentment and hate, on pettiness and meanness until this wonderful gift of the Creator is washed away.

And then there's the soul. Clearly enough, this was the ultimate issue of Jesus' story. The decisions we make regarding our bodies and our minds combine to shape decisions for the soul. Eternal decisions.

If this house of ours weren't worth much—if our bodies and brains and will and personalities were trivial things, to be thrown together one day and torn down the next—if that were so, it wouldn't much matter what foundation we might choose. But the stuff that constitutes you and me is utterly invaluable. There is no other soul like yours or mine, no other life that can replace it. We'd better build this house on a foundation that will survive the inevitable storms because it's the only one we can get.

That's why Jesus said some people are fools. They just don't realize the value of the house that God has put in their charge.

CHAPTER 2

The Man Who Talked with His Soul

LUKE 12:13-21: Someone in the crowd said to him, "Teacher, tell my brother to divide the family inheritance with me." But he said to him, "Friend, who set me to be a judge or arbitrator over you?" And he said to them, "Take care! Be on your guard against all kinds of greed; for one's life does not consist in the abundance of possessions." Then he told them a parable: "The land of a rich man produced abundantly. And he thought to himself, 'What should I do, for I have no place to store my crops?' Then he said, 'I will do this: I will pull down my barns and build larger ones, and there I will store all my grain and my goods. And I will say to my soul, Soul, you have ample goods laid up for many years; relax, eat, drink, be merry.' But God said to him, 'You fool! This very night your life is being demanded of you. And the things you have prepared, whose will they be?' So it is with those who store up treasures for themselves but are not rich toward God."

I want to tell you about a remarkable man. He was remarkable in many ways—in his business instincts, in his financial success, and in the conversations he held. Especially, in his conversations; and then, ironically—quite in contrast to his conversations—in the way his story ended.

I don't know his name because the Bible doesn't mention it. He was a character in one of Jesus' parables, and Jesus very rarely mentioned names in his parables. Jesus called him "a rich man," and near the end of the brief story, Jesus said that God called this man a fool. Since the man comes to us in a parable, he is a fictitious character; but without a doubt Jesus knew somebody like him. So did many of the people who were listening to Jesus. This is one of the reasons Jesus' parables so faithfully caught the attention of the casual crowds, because the people said to themselves, "I know a fellow just like that." If Jesus' parables had been put into movies, it would have been necessary to run a line across the screen, "Any resemblance between the characters depicted herein and anyone living or dead is purely coincidental." Except, of course, that it wasn't so coincidental. So we read the stories nearly twenty centuries later and know that Jesus was talking about real people, people we know. Indeed, at times we confess, in uneasy honesty, that he was talking about us, ourselves.

Jesus got into this story because one day a man in the crowd asked him to intervene in a siblings' quarrel regarding the family inheritance. I'm fascinated by this request. It probably indicates the variety of matters that people brought to Jesus, seeking his insight, help, or influence. After all, the crowds saw him as a teacher in a society that honored knowledge; and they saw him as a wise man in a world that looked upon wisdom as the highest good. Jesus refused to intervene in the family argument, then added a warning: Be on your guard against greed, because "one's life does not consist in the abundance of possessions" (Luke 12:15).

Then Jesus told his story. "The land of a rich man," he said, "produced abundantly" (Luke 12:16). Immediately we know several things. The man is already rich, perhaps by inheritance, perhaps by his management skills, probably by a combination of the two. And he's a landowner. From time immemorial, the secret of continuing wealth is in getting good land and holding it unless and until it's more profitable to sell it. His land is *good* land; it produces "abundantly." Jesus' listeners must have heard this part of the story with unfeigned envy. If you've been to the Middle East, you know that it seems like much of the land is filled with rocks and stones. Big ones, little ones, rough ones, smooth ones. That part of the world doesn't have much land that brings forth "abundantly." So this is an exceedingly fortunate man. He has the kind of land farmers dream of, and he knows what to do with it. Some people get good land and still don't produce much. Not this man. His land is lush to the eye. Walking by his fields is a delight. I don't know how he did it. Perhaps he hired agricultural specialists. Perhaps he brought together a great team of workers, the way a premier coach surrounds himself with top-rank assistants. It could be, too, that he paid his skilled workers well, so that he got a high level of loyalty from them. Whatever his secret, this man knew how to make farming pay.

Or perhaps, just perhaps, he was very fortunate. He may have inherited good land from his father and grandfather, and the winds may have favored his land with the best passing clouds, and the locust plagues may have followed another course, so that all life's issues seemed to conspire to his benefit. One way or another, this man was rich, and he was steadily getting still richer.

Well, this presented a problem. He looked at his prosperity and said, "What am I going to do? I have no more room to store my crops." And being a bright man, he came to a sensible conclusion: "I will pull down my barns and build larger ones" (Luke 12:18).

This man deserves a visiting lectureship at the Harvard School of Business Administration or the Wharton School of Finance. Wal-Mart surely has a vice-presidency awaiting him. See how well he would do with our present shopping-mall mentality. We follow his reasoning all across America. In towns of just about any size, when a mall thrives, some other financial genius buys several hundred acres just up or down the road and builds a *greater* mall. And if the first mall eventually deteriorates into a collection of marginal businesses and empty storefronts, who cares? "I will tear down my mall and build a greater one!" This man may have lived two thousand years ago, but he knew the principles by which we operate today. It's really quite astonishing.

But I haven't told you the most important thing about this man. Listen to what else the man says: "And I will say to my soul, Soul, you have ample goods laid up for many years; relax, eat, drink, be merry" (Luke 12:19).

I told you he was a remarkable man. It's not simply that he was a rich man who knew how to make still more money. He was a person who talked to his soul! He didn't talk simply to his glands or to his gullet, as so many of us do; not even to his bank account or to his tax return, as a financial genius would be expected to do. He didn't settle even for talking to his mind, a practice for which I would commend him. He's still better than that. He talked to his *soul.* "*Soul,*" he said. This is a spiritual man. I admit that I'm impressed.

And in the next breath I have to say that in this quality, too, our man is a twenty-first century man. He was a spiritual person, and we have so many spiritual people today. One hears it nearly every day, especially if we listen to the television talk shows or if we read the entertainment section of the newspaper or popular magazines. "I'm not religious," the postmodern person carefully disclaims, "but I'm very spiritual." Some of the largest bookstores are caught up with this mood. Where once they had a Religion section, they now have a section on Spiritual Writings. There's a quasi-secular book club dedicated to this genre, if I may call it that. I venture that only for several short periods in the nineteenth century has there been a time in America when there was such enthusiasm for spirituality. I won't try to distinguish between the different interpretations of the word *spirituality* because the definitions currently are almost as numerous as the persons who use the word. I just want you to understand that the rich man in Jesus' story was a very spiritual person, and that in this respect, too, he would be quite at home in our world.

I've spent so much of my life in the world of the parish pastor that I can't help imagining how the rich man in this parable would sound in our day. I picture him coming to his pastor's church office. "Pastor," he says, "I want to talk over a matter that concerns my soul. As you may have noticed, my business is doing well. Indeed, *very* well. So well, in fact, that I think I have to expand." Now at this moment, in our day, the man wouldn't say, as did the person in Jesus' story, "I've been talking with my soul about this." Rather, he would say something like, "Well, I've been praying about this." At this point the pastor embraces him and tells him how wonderful it is that he's such a spiritual man. Later in the week, at a luncheon with ministerial colleagues, the pastor brags just a bit about this man. Perhaps he even hints that the man's spirituality is a result of the pastor's own penetrating preaching.

But see how differently God views this whole matter. "But God said to him," Jesus tells us, "'You fool! This very night your life is being demanded of you. And the things you have prepared, whose will they be?'" (Luke 12:20). Read this verse very carefully. When you put it all together, you realize that God was saying, "You damned fool." This, after all, is what the sentence amounts to. I say this carefully, because I have just used a theological term—"damned"—that has been so thoroughly taken over by the secular culture that when it is used correctly, it shocks and offends people. *Damned* has to do with eternal matters, not the petty stuff of thoughtless anger. But how can it be that a person who is so spiritual that he talks with his soul would end up being described by God as a fool; indeed, as a damned fool? How can this be? A great preacher of another generation, Ernest Fremont Tittle, put it well. "Certainly a man is a *fool* if, having made a lot of money, he can think of nothing better to do than make more money" (Ernest Fremont Tittle, *The Gospel According to Luke* [New York: Harper & Brothers Publishers, 1951], page 136).

But still, how can a person be so spiritual and still be a fool?

On the surface, the situation seems self-contradictory. But in real life, it happens very easily. Let's look at this man's case. I must start by being honest with you. His first problem is that he's rich. It is very difficult to be rich and still keep your balance. And "rich" is defined many different ways. For this man, it was farmland, crops, and accumulated monetary wealth. For a college student or a professional educator, "rich" is likely to mean a clever, inquisitive mind. For far too many of us, it lies in the quest for the "perfect" body, along with eternally youthful good looks. And for a preacher, it can mean having the ability to put together a sermon that makes someone say, "That's probably the best sermon I've ever heard." Believe me, there are many ways to be rich; rich enough to be a fool. And hear me: *It's hard to be rich and not be a fool.* Because when one is rich, one loses certain crucial ties with reality.

Another thing. This man had a serious "I" problem. Listen to him. In my Bible (the *New Revised Standard Version*), he speaks sixty words, and eleven of them are *I* or *my*. And all of them—every single one!—are concerned with his own welfare. This may be a spiritual man, but he is one of the smallest men you'll ever meet. Whatever about him is spiritual is consumed by his self-absorption.

As I read this man's story, as told by Jesus in this penetrating parable, something occurs to me. So many of the villains in Jesus' parables were spiritual people. The Pharisee who went into the temple to pray was very spiritual; one of the most spiritual persons I've ever met (see Luke 18:9-14). And in the story of the good Samaritan, the priest and the Levite were the spiritual people, by the very nature of their daily work (see Luke 10:25-37). Or consider the parable of the father and his two sons, the parable we often refer to as "the prodigal son"; there, too, the older brother is the spiritual one. He's the one who says to his father, "I have never disobeyed your command." You never saw a more law-abiding declaration than that. He was, by our usual definitions, a good, spiritual person (see Luke 15:11-32).

Come to think of it, it was the appointed spiritual leaders of Jesus' time who engineered his arrest and crucifixion. The Roman government and its soldiers carried it out, but it was professional religionists who set it up.

Which goes to show that a person can know all the facts, yet miss the point. We can reason logically, yet come to the wrong conclusion. We can say all the right words while having a wrong heart.

Let me be specific. We can be Bible scholars without letting the teachings of the Bible touch our hearts. We can argue the cause of our particular religious point of view, but remain mean and small inside. Yes, and it's possible even to pray, and while praying move farther and farther from God, because we employ prayer only to enlist God's power for our own selfish ends. It isn't enough to baptize our prayer at its conclusion by saying, "In Jesus' name" unless the prayer is brought captive to the spirit of our Lord.

So what hope is there, someone says? If someone who is so spiritual that he talks with his soul nevertheless misses, and if it's possible to use even spiritual devices in unworthy ways, what hope is there? How can we escape the pitfalls that caught this remarkable businessman, this man who talked with his soul?

I'm happy to tell you that the solution is really quite simple. You'll find the solution in the things this rich man *left out.* For one, spiritual as he was, he left out *God.* Can you imagine that? If you'll think about it for a minute, you'll realize that this is the missing ingredient in a great deal of contemporary spirituality. It concentrates so heavily on the person, and what "spirituality" will do for that person's job, personality, relationships, or success. And that's the way it was with the man in Jesus' parable. He talked to his soul, but he didn't let God in on the conversation.

That was the first part of his problem, that he omitted God. The other thing he left out was other people. There's not a word in his speech, and apparently not a thought in his mind, for other people. Believe me, any spirituality that has no room for other people is a complete fraud.

That's all that was wrong with this remarkable man. He talked with his soul, but he forgot God and he forgot other people. The poor fool! The poor, *damned* fool.

CHAPTER 3

What Chance Does an Average Sinner Have?

LUKE 7:36-48: One of the Pharisees asked Jesus to eat with him, and he went into the Pharisee's house and took his place at the table. And a woman in the city, who was a sinner, having learned that he was eating in the Pharisee's house, brought an alabaster jar of ointment. She stood behind him at his feet, weeping, and began to bathe his feet with her tears and to dry them with her hair. Then she continued kissing his feet and anointing them with the ointment. Now when the Pharisee who had invited him saw it, he said to himself, "If this man were a prophet, he would have known who and what kind of woman this is who is touching him—that she is a sinner." Jesus spoke up and said to him, "Simon, I have something to say to you." "Teacher," he replied, "speak." "A certain creditor had two debtors; one owed five hundred denarii, and the other fifty. When they could not pay, he canceled the debts for both of them. Now which of them will love him more?" Simon answered, "I suppose the one for whom he canceled the greater debt." And Jesus said to him, "You have judged rightly." Then turning toward the woman, he said to Simon, "Do you see this woman? I entered your house; you gave me no water for my feet, but she has bathed my feet with her tears and dried them with her hair. You gave me no kiss, but from the time I came in she has not stopped kissing my feet. You did not anoint my head with oil, but she has anointed my feet with ointment. Therefore, I tell you, her sins, which were many, have been forgiven; hence she has shown great love. But the one to whom little is forgiven, loves little." Then he said to her, "Your sins are forgiven."

I am an Iowa boy, so I didn't have the privilege of growing up with great Southern storytellers. Thus, my first venture into America's southland was a revelation and a delight. Not only were the preachers storytellers, so was almost everyone else; at least anyone over the age of fifty. The first time I preached at the Tabernacle Camp Meeting in West Tennessee, I thought I had moved into some kind of oral-tradition heaven. A story didn't have to be new. Someone was likely to say, "Alsey, tell us about the time you and Sue were coming back from Europe," and everyone settled in to hear a story most of them had heard many times before. But most of the time, the stories sprang up as commentary on whatever course the conversation was taking. "That reminds me," someone would say, and I would know that in a moment the issue would get an irresistible point.

That's what Jesus did with the parables. So often the parables grew out of a remark from one of Jesus' opponents or from a question by a seeker. So it was with the parable of two debtors. The parable is so brief (just thirty-six words in the Bible before me) that one could easily miss it; and all the more so since it comes in the midst of a dramatic incident. I'll have to tell you the incident in order for you to appreciate the parable, because the point of the parable is in the incident.

A Pharisee named Simon had asked Jesus to eat with him. I sense that the dinner was a social occasion with several guests; and as I start reading the story, I feel that Simon is probably a rather nice sort. Not too many Pharisees invited Jesus for dinner; his hosts were usually tax collectors and sinners. Of course it's possible that Simon considered Jesus some sort of social trophy, a kind of living conversation piece who would be thoroughly analyzed by Simon's friends after he had left the gathering. But I don't want to feel that way about Simon. I want to give him the benefit of the doubt.

But the dinner took a peculiar turn. In pleasant weather, the eating area in nicer first-century homes was in an open courtyard; and when a respected teacher was a guest, people often stopped by to listen in on the conversation. They were not intruding by doing so; as a matter of fact, such eavesdropping was a kind of compliment to the family who could entertain such a guest. Jesus may have been a bit notorious from a Pharisee's point of view, but among the general public he was very popular. We don't know how many people had gathered at the outskirts of the table, but we know about one because she was soon the center of attention.

Luke tells us that she was "a sinner." This is a gentle euphemism. She was a prostitute, and apparently an easily recognized one. She came to where Jesus was reclining at the table, his feet stretched out and his sandals removed, planning to anoint his feet with ointment from an alabaster jar. But the woman was weeping so profusely that before she could open the jar of ointment, her tears began bathing Jesus' feet. She had intended to show her gratitude with the ointment; now she was simply making a mess of things. Her act of adoration had become like all the rest of her life, a confusing embarrassment. Poor soul, she couldn't even say thank you without stumbling over it. Now there was no way to dry the Teacher's feet, so she made matters still worse by beginning to wipe his feet with her hair.

Nothing could have been more inappropriate. In the Jewish first-century world, a woman bound up her hair on her wedding day, never again to be seen publicly with her hair unbound. Even a woman of the streets knew better than to unbind her hair publicly; and now to approach the Teacher in such an intimate way was unthinkable. As a matter of fact, even our quite promiscuous times would be undone if a woman, good or bad, approached a man at a dinner party in some similar fashion, and all the more so if the man were a public personality. The major media outlets would scramble to get those pictures.

And then the woman was so overcome that she couldn't stop. At last she began spilling out the ointment, what had been the original reason for her trip, all the while kissing Jesus' feet.

Jesus did nothing to reprove her. He didn't withdraw his feet. He seemed unembarrassed by her display. This bothered Simon the Pharisee even more than what the woman had done. Luke says that Simon said to himself, "If this man were a prophet, he would have known who and what kind of woman this is who is touching him—that she is a sinner" (Luke 7:39). John's Gospel says in another connection that Jesus "needed no one to testify about anyone; for he himself knew what was in everyone" (John 2:25). In this instance I doubt that Jesus needed any special discernment to read Simon's mind. The expression on Simon's face was probably such that you or I would have gotten the message, too. Besides, the woman had come to look like her profession; she had lived so long with darkness that the shadows of her life were written into her poor countenance.

"Simon," Jesus said, "I have something to say to you." "Teacher," Simon answered, "speak." The brevity of Simon's response is telling. Perhaps his breath has been so taken away that he can't say more than two words. I won't smile too broadly because I might have been just as undone. And here it is that Jesus offers his spur-of-the-moment, few-sentences parable.

"A certain creditor had two debtors; one owed five hundred denarii, and the other fifty. When they could not pay, he canceled the debts for both of them. Now which of them will love him more?" (Luke 7:41-42). Your Bible's footnote probably tells you that a *denarius* was, in that first-century world, a day's wage for a laborer. And of course a day's wage was essentially just enough to maintain a common worker and his family for a day, because theirs was a very marginal way of life. To owe someone fifty denarii meant that with a little luck here and there and some exceeding care, you might over a period of time pay off your debt. But five hundred denarii? This was hopeless. One would have to work a year and a half and put all the labor simply to the paying of the debt, while finding some other means of daily subsistence.

So Jesus' question for Simon was, as they say, a no-brainer. Simon's answer, as reflected in our English translation, says as much: "I suppose the one for whom he canceled the greater debt." Simon must have felt it was a trick question; so to protect himself from embarrassment by an awkward response, he said, essentially, "What other answer could there be?"

Jesus answered, "You have judged rightly." But Jesus didn't stop there. Most of the time, Jesus didn't "apply" his parables. He usually left it to his hearers to make the application to their own lives. Unlike some contemporary preachers, Jesus didn't beat folks over the head with his point. Indeed, sometimes he seemed almost cavalier in the way he left it to them to apply a story to themselves if they chose to do so. But this time Jesus left nothing to Simon's imagination. I don't know why he was so direct with Simon. Perhaps it's because Simon was a rather good sort, so Jesus extended himself to make the point clear. On the other hand, perhaps Simon was so spiritually obtuse that Jesus thought he'd have to spell out the issue or Simon would never get it.

Jesus did so by directing Simon's attention to the woman. Jesus said, "Do you see this woman? I entered your house; you gave me no water for my feet, but she has bathed my feet with her tears and dried them with her hair. You gave me no kiss, but from the time I came in she has not stopped kissing my feet. You did not anoint my head with oil, but she has anointed my feet with ointment. Therefore, I tell you, her sins, which were many, have been forgiven; hence she has shown great love. But the one to whom little is forgiven, loves little" (Luke 7:44-47). Jesus then told the woman her sins were forgiven, a statement that upset the dinner guests still more; "Who is this," they muttered to one another, "who even forgives sins?" At which point Jesus diverted the issue in still another direction, by acknowledging the power of the woman's faith: "Your faith has saved you; go in peace" (Luke 7:50).

I'm anxious to examine Simon's situation, since it probably bears some resemblance to issues that concern you and me. But first let's look at Simon's conduct. Simon is a person who knows correct social procedures. Indeed, any slave in that culture knew what was expected in matters of hospitality, to say nothing of a Pharisee who prided himself on proper conduct. A good host in the first-century Middle Eastern world greeted a guest (especially someone as distinguished as a rabbi) by placing a hand on the shoulder and giving a kiss of peace. Then, cool water was poured over the sandal-clad feet, for comfort, cleanliness, and courtesy. Finally, some perfume was touched on the guest's head as a signal of affection and respect.

Simon had ignored all of these conventional courtesies, a quite unbelievable violation of the social mores. Much of our contemporary cultural pattern is so casual that it's hard to make a proper comparison; but I suppose it is as if someone were to invite a major public personality for dinner, then fail even to say upon the person's arrival, "May I offer you a chair?" Jesus had been insulted. It seems to me that he would have been justified in excusing himself and leaving. That is, for all practical purposes Simon was being patently denigrating, which seems so out of character for Simon. One wonders exactly what he had in mind. Did he intend to humiliate Jesus before his other guests? Was he seeking to belittle him? Or was he simply thoughtless? If so, the woman made up for the neglect. She bathed Jesus' feet not with water but with her tears; she replaced the formality of a kiss of peace with the kissing of Jesus' feet; and instead of a touch of perfume, she poured out an expensive alabaster jar of ointment. The contrast could not have been more dramatic. Jesus' summary is quite matter of fact: The woman has been forgiven much, so she "has shown great love." But someone (like Simon!) "to whom little is forgiven, loves little" (Luke 7:47).

Obviously Jesus was reflecting Simon's impression of himself when he spoke of someone "to whom little is forgiven," but Simon had no right to think of himself as having little that needed to be forgiven. The climactic day of Jewish forgiveness, the Day of Atonement, didn't offer gradations of sin; sin was sin, with no gentle nod to the respectable. Jesus was also indicating the different ways in which sinful Simon and the sinful woman perceived him. For Simon, Jesus was a dinner guest, a currently popular rabbi. Simon didn't really need him very much, except as part of a social occasion. For the woman, Jesus was crucial. In her troubled life, he was a singular refuge.

Nothing in Luke's report suggests that the woman was asking Jesus for forgiveness, but as the story ends, Jesus says to her, "Your sins are forgiven." Did Jesus speak these words simply out of compassion for her need? Or was the woman's manner itself a mute appeal for forgiveness? Perhaps her actions articulated more clearly than any spoken words. The apostle Peter spoke a sentence, "You are the Messiah, the Son of the living God" (Matthew 16:16), on which Jesus said the church would be built. As I see it, the woman spoke the same theme with ointment, kisses, and tears, and with her message she entered the kingdom of Heaven.

But the parable leaves me with a problem. If, as Jesus said, "the one to whom little is forgiven, loves little," what hope is there for us garden-variety sinners? What chance does an average sinner have? When one hears the stories of those who have been saved from drug addiction or redeemed from a life of crime, the person who has gone directly from Sunday school to youth conferences to continuing church membership seems almost like a second-class citizen in the world of the Spirit. In a church where I was pastor, we once had a weekend youth retreat with a man who had lived very recklessly before his conversion. The mother of one of our young people complained to me afterwards; she feared her son might feel he'd better explore sin more widely so that he could enjoy his religion better.

Indeed, one gets something of that feeling from Jesus' parable of the two brothers in the fifteenth chapter of Luke's Gospel. The older brother complains that no one ever gave *him* a party. His father explains that he could have had a party at any time. No further word is spoken, but I suspect the older brother had a feeling that there had never been an occasion in his life that called for a party; after all, he had always stayed at home, so there were no homecomings to celebrate.

So does that mean that we "average sinners" can never really have the same sense of redemption the more dramatic converts know? Did Simon ever have a chance to feel greatly forgiven? I sometimes remind those who are Sunday school bred that they escape the scars that mark those whose conversion happens after great spiritual trauma, but still the question remains: Is the "average sinner" out on the edge of heaven's better parties?

Not as Charles Wesley would see it—or Teresa of Avila—or a host of people I've known over the years, but whose privacy I have no right to invade by mentioning their names. Charles Wesley could write "O for a thousand tongues to sing my great Redeemer's praise," which sounds as if he had been delivered from some of life's worst pits, but in truth he was a model son raised in the home of an Anglican rector; Charles Wesley never walked on the wild side. Teresa of Avila, one of Catholicism's canonized saints, wanted from girlhood to be a nun and never deviated from that course. The excitement of her walk with God was as great as that of Saint Augustine or Francis of Assisi, both of whom were pursued by God down hazardous roads.

So what is the difference between John Newton, the libertine and slave trader who wrote "Amazing Grace," and Charles Wesley, the lifelong seeker of goodness who gave us "Hark! the Herald Angels Sing"? Just this, I think. John

Newton knew the grace of God by his salvation from sin experienced, while Charles Wesley knew it from the possibility of sin escaped. Wesley was wise enough to know that under other circumstances he would quite surely have been the worst of offenders. He could, indeed, look at any pathetic wretch and say, "There, but for the grace of God, go I," because he knew he had the same capacity for sin, the same potential for self-destruction.

That is to say—spiritually speaking some of us are like the accident victim who, in gurney and bandages, says from the hospital bed, "I'm just glad to be alive," while others of us are like the person who comes home in the evening, still shaken, to say, "Just a split second today, and I would have been a goner. I'm just glad to be alive."

They both have reason to be grateful. Equal reason, in fact. Take it from me, a Sunday school boy who knew before he was eleven that he would be a preacher. I just made it! By the grace of God, I made it. I know, in some measure, from what I've been saved. So strike up a homecoming party. My name may be Simon, but I have been forgiven *much.*

CHAPTER 4

The Importance of Downward Mobility

LUKE 14:7-14: When he noticed how the guests chose the places of honor, he told them a parable. "When you are invited by someone to a wedding banquet, do not sit down at the place of honor, in case someone more distinguished than you has been invited by your host; and the host who invited both of you may come and say to you, 'Give this person your place' and then in disgrace you would start to take the lowest place. But when you are invited, go and sit down at the lowest place, so that when your host comes, he may say to you, 'Friend, move up higher'; then you will be honored in the presence of all who sit at the table with you. For all who exalt themselves will be humbled, and those who humble themselves will be exalted."

He said also to the one who had invited him, "When you give a luncheon or a dinner, do not invite your friends or your brothers or your relatives or rich neighbors, in case they may invite you in return, and you would be repaid. But when you give a banquet, invite the poor, the crippled, the lame, and the blind. And you will be blessed, because they cannot repay you, for you will be repaid at the resurrection of the righteous."

If I were to discuss my personality defects with a psychiatrist, I'm sure the conference would at some point touch on a social experience that occurred when I was seven years old. I thought about it again during my last visit to my hometown—a visit I make almost every year. I stood near the ungraceful duplex where we lived that childhood year and considered the house catty-cornered across from me; a relatively modest house, but decidedly better than what ours had been. It held particular distinction in our neighborhood because the family had a refrigerator—the only one in the area. One summer day they even gave an ice cube to each of us boys. It was an event but also a letdown; the cube didn't compare with the slivers of ice we scrounged from the ice wagon that served the neighborhood, perhaps partly because the pieces from the ice wagon weren't as pure as the refrigerator cube and therefore had more flavor.

I digress, but not without purpose. You understand from what I've just said that the house across the street represented more substance than the other houses on the corner of Fifteenth and Virginia. So when the owners' son (let's call him Robert) invited me to have the evening meal at their home, I was both thrilled and afraid. My mother agreed that this would be nice, and with her very lively sense of middle-class propriety, said that I would bring dessert for the meal—watermelon.

So we sat down to the kitchen table in their home, and something went wrong. Even today I have no idea of exactly what happened. I remember that their dishes were matched, which ours (on weekdays) were not; and that they served pork chops with mashed potatoes and gravy. The fragrance of the pork chops is with me yet. But for some reason, my plate was left bare. Robert and his parents ate happily while I responded to their conversation and played with my fork. I don't know if, in my timidity, I refused the food when it was passed to me, or whether there was a misunderstanding and I was expected to bring my own main course. I only know that I had nothing until the watermelon—my contribution to the meal—was served.

Since then I have been the guest at thousands of meals

and have sat at the head table at hundreds of banquets, but that night at Fifteenth and Virginia established my lifelong conviction that I don't want to be anywhere where I may not be wanted.

So I read with poignant interest the advice Jesus gave his followers through a little story. He and his disciples were at some sort of social occasion. This happened often; Jesus was a popular dinner guest, partly because he was a public personality and partly because people so much enjoyed his presence. Jesus noticed with amusement the way the guests elbowed their way to the places of honor at the table. Mel Brooks is credited with giving us the line, "That's it, baby, when you['ve] got it, flaunt it," but as with many classic lines, Brooks was simply codifying a practice as old as Cain's jealousy for his brother Abel. The advice has more possibilities in our time because we have so many more areas of possible puffery. In a world where attainments were measured in the number of sheep owned or the size of the corn crop, not many could flaunt; and it was easy to check the integrity of the flaunting. But today, when there are so many measures of imagined success, almost everyone has something to flaunt—to the point, indeed, of absurdity. But the absurdity doesn't stop folks from doing the flaunting.

Observing human nature at work, Jesus told a story. Uncharacteristically, he began the story with advice. When you're invited to a wedding banquet (one of the very special social events in that first-century world), don't sit down in the place of honor; it's just possible that someone of greater distinction may be coming. If that happens, you'll suffer major embarrassment because you'll be deposed in favor of the preferred guest. Instead, "go and sit down at the lowest place, so that when your host comes, he may say to you, 'Friend, move up higher' " (Luke 14:10). If that happens, Jesus said, "You will be honored in the presence of all who sit at the table with you." Jesus concluded, "For all who exalt themselves will be humbled, and those who humble themselves will be exalted" (Luke 14:10-11).

So what's this parable all about? At the least, it's good social counsel. In the banquet of life there is almost always someone who merits a higher seat than I do. So much depends on the occasion and the standards by which the "guests" are evaluated. I was at a gathering of scholars not long ago. I dabble at the edges of the world of scholarship (remote edges, to be honest), so I recognize some achievers in the scholars' world. I found I knew hardly anyone at this gathering, but I also discovered that some of them were mightily impressed with one another. I was rather glad for them, even if also amused. During my days as a pastor, I gave the invocation for a wondrous variety of occasions, some of them quite obscure. I learned, however, that there was no occasion so obscure that it didn't bring a sense of importance to some who were there. Wherever one goes, there's a chance one will be upstaged by someone else. When the United Matchbook Collectors of the World (yes, I made that up) convene, the patriarch of the group will get more attention than the visiting CEO of a Fortune 500 company, unless that CEO is also a Matchbook Collector. Between you and me, all of us live in quite small worlds.

So yes, this is good social counsel. We're well advised not to be unduly in awe of ourselves and to walk with humility lest someone or some occasion inflict humility upon us. And in truth, there is in all of us a certain hunger for attention, acknowledgment, and preferment. For some, unfortunately, the hunger is ravenous. There's something pathetic in those persons who, no matter how much attention they're paid, are always seeking still another compliment or still another evidence of achievement. But all of us desire some measure of recognition. I've met a few folks who denied any such desire, but I discovered that they wanted to be recognized for this lack of desire.

Indeed, in this story Jesus gives a kind of tacit endorsement to the pleasure of recognition. If you don't promote yourself, he says, you will enjoy being promoted by others; and if you humble yourself, you will be exalted. Such promotion and exaltation should be seen as by-products of life and not as ends in themselves. And they are benefits much more befitting when bestowed by others. When gotten by our own seeking, they take on an unpleasant flavor. I'm reminding you of something you already know. All of us have said of certain individuals something like, "He'd be easier to like if he just weren't so in love with himself."

In a very practical sense, the event Jesus described in the setting of a wedding feast goes on daily at another level of life. When people exalt themselves, we begin looking for flaws that will diminish them. We do it either in conversation with others, as we slowly dismantle the self-promoter's standing, or simply within our own minds, as we list the reasons this person isn't as wonderful as he or she thinks himself or herself to be. So it is that we adjust the wedding's seating arrangements in the ballroom of our minds.

At the least, then, Jesus' little parable is good, everyday social counsel. It's a sound rule for people who want to get along with others and for those who would like to move up in business or politics. The newspaper and television analysts tell us as much every week as they report on political, entertainment, or sports personalities who are liked for their pleasantness or disliked for their arrogance. And it's quite possible this is the lesson Jesus intended to convey in this parable. We are sometimes so inclined to limit Jesus to teachings of eternal significance that we forget that he was beloved by his contemporaries as a rabbi, and the rabbis were notable for their common sense and for their very down-to-earth counsel. I'm really quite sure that in Jesus' daily discourses he sometimes offered insights on relatively inconsequential matters; just as in our day if he were among us, he might have an opinion about what yesterday's quarterback should have done when it was third down with eight yards to go for a first down. For Jesus, eternity was always in view, just as it should be for us; but there was also work to be done, errands to be run, and minutiae to be tended to. So of course it's possible that Jesus was simply giving good, rabbinical advice.

And it could have been commonsense advice with a further philosophical touch. Jesus might have been reminding us that there is no real fulfillment in self-promotion. If all the good things that are said about us in our eulogies are things we wrote in preparation for the event, it's just as well we won't be there to hear it. If the prominence we have at life's banquet tables has been gotten by elbowing our way, even while others have been contemptuous of our position, we haven't gained much.

But is there more to the parable? Does it end here? If so, it's good material for a book that will show us how to win friends and influence people. But I can't help feeling there's more to it than that. When I place this parable in the context of Jesus' life, I'm certain he was giving more than Rule Number Six in "The Thirteen Secrets for Sure Success." This one who said that if we want to save our lives, we will have to be ready to lose them, and who told those who wanted to follow him that to do so they would have to take up their cross daily—surely he's giving us more than good social or business counsel, or even insights for inner peace. And especially, since this comes in that portion of Luke's Gospel when Jesus had "set his face to go to Jerusalem" (Luke 9:51). As Jesus headed toward the Crucifixion, he often seemed impatient with pettiness and needless distraction. It's especially hard, in this setting, to imagine Jesus being trifling in his teaching.

Of this I'm very sure: Jesus wanted his disciples—and any others who would hear—to realize that in this life of ours very few achievements matter except goodness and godliness. And when we come to the ultimate banquet of eternity, goodness and godliness will be the total measure. It's quite absurd to imagine ourselves greeted in heaven by a God who says, "I see that you were president of the Amundsville Rotary Club! How wonderful!" Or even less, that God might say, "I'm so impressed; you had a twenty-seven-foot boat and a silver service that was the envy of your neighborhood!" Hardly! God will be looking for more than where we were seated at the last wedding dinner or community honors banquet. In truth, everything about Jesus' life and teaching is a recommendation for downward mobility. No one could be less at home in our "if-you've-got-it, flaunt-it" culture than Jesus.

As Jesus continued his comments, he gave still more insight on downward mobility. When you give a luncheon, he told his host, "do not invite your friends or your brothers or your relatives or rich neighbors, in case they may invite you in return, and you would be repaid. But when you give a banquet, invite the poor, the crippled, the lame, and the blind. And you will be blessed, because they cannot repay you, for you will be repaid at the resurrection of the righteous" (Luke 14:12-14).

Obviously, Jesus isn't impressed with our usual idea for a dinner party. The worst of us invite people on the basis of what they can do for us, which is a rather larcenous attitude toward the social life. The rest of us invite our family and the people we like. Isn't that what a party is for? And I think Jesus would answer, "Yes, if you see a party as entirely earthbound. But if you perceive a party as having some eternal dimensions, then you will want to reevaluate your guest list. You'll want to invite some people who rarely get to parties."

This gets rather complicated. What will your neighbors think of you if they see several nondescript cars pull up to your home for a party or if you bring to your home some people who never get into a neighborhood like yours? Or what will your business associates think if they see you with an unlikely luncheon guest at a popular restaurant? I still remember my favorite high-school teacher warning me that I was endangering my standing with the faculty by my friendship with Bill. In time, Bill became a Christian through our friendship, but there's no guarantee for a successful ending to all our stories; and without a doubt, my teacher's counsel was not only earnest but well-founded.

I'm not suggesting that we should never have parties for our friends or that we should make all our social occasions into holy recruitments or welfare projects. But I'm quite sure Jesus is trying to tell us several things about our social practices. For sure, he reminds us that the purpose of life is not preferment; we aren't on this planet simply to gain the highest seats, the most offices, or the largest plunder. And he would also tell us that there is more to life than *this* life. Whatever we gain from a celebration, whether it is advancement in the social register or simply the enjoyment of friendship, we should remember that there is also the question of a day somewhere down the road, a day Jesus called "the resurrection of the righteous." That's an occasion that will put any current table-seating arrangement very much in the shade!

In other words, Jesus is offering a wholey different rule for social conduct (which includes business-social conduct and church-social conduct). He is making a case for downward mobility; a case that the apostle Paul clarified later when he wrote to the Christians at Philippi that we should have the same mind that was in Christ Jesus, who, "though he was in the form of God . . . humbled himself / and became obedient to the point of death— / even death on a cross." And because he did this, God exalted him, "and gave him the name / that is above every name" (Philippians 2:5-9). That is, Jesus knew what he was talking about when he recommended downward mobility.

This puts a whole new take on our social life, our business life, and perhaps even our church life. And we will probably never fully grasp Jesus' teaching on downward mobility as we go about life's various banquet tables and their honors unless we picture a banquet table where God is sitting at the head. Only then will we get the order straight. Only then will we fully understand the holy principle of downward mobility.

But in the meanwhile, we ought to work at it.

CHAPTER 5

The Danger of Being Good and Empty

MATTHEW 12:43-45: When the unclean spirit has gone out of a person, it wanders through waterless regions looking for a resting place, but it finds none. Then it says, "I will return to my house from which I came." When it comes, it finds it empty, swept, and put in order. Then it goes and brings along seven other spirits more evil than itself, and they enter and live there; and the last state of that person is worse than the first. So will it be also with this evil generation.

Let me begin with a safe statement. *Everybody, or almost everybody, wants to be good.* We may not want it badly enough to work at it. We don't necessarily want it all the time. We may want goodness for wrong reasons. And of course it's very possible that our definition of *good* is inadequate or self-serving. But almost everyone wants to be good. If someone wants sincerely to be bad, we consider that person a sociopath. Such an attitude is outside the realm of reasonable human thought and conduct.

Here's a second safe statement. It's something of a variation on the first, yet different. *Everyone desires what we like to call "the good life."* We prefer to be healthy, to have a certain degree of economic security, and to enjoy some measure of comfort. The definition of these terms—especially *economic security* and *comfort*—varies a good deal, depending on one's background and one's level of expectation, but most of us desire such a "good life." When someone chooses instead to be self-destructive, we judge that probably the person is mentally ill.

Now since everyone, or almost everyone, wants to be good, one wonders why the world isn't better off than it is. After all, goodness isn't a product in short supply, of the sort that *your* becoming good means there won't be enough for *me*; to the contrary, the better *you* are, the easier it is for *me* to be good. One would think therefore that with so many of us wanting to be good, our planet would be tilted wonderfully toward perfection. But all of us know that this isn't so, which brings me to the point of our parable. I have to tell you that goodness is not enough, nor is the proverbial "good life" enough.

Here's the story, as Jesus told it. There was a person who had an "unclean spirit." Jesus didn't describe the condition further. I'm inclined to think that having an unclean spirit was not the same thing as what the New Testament calls demon possession. Unlike those instances, this man isn't described as being violent or presenting a danger to either himself or his neighbors. The scripture simply says that there was some uncleanness in him. This is graphic language. I'm sure it means more than simply a particular instance of moral failure. The term "unclean spirit" suggests a way of life that comes from an inner predisposition.

Then, somehow, he was cleaned up. The unclean spirit had "gone out" of him. Again, Jesus doesn't give us any details. Maybe the man turned over a new leaf. Perhaps he took the first-century equivalent of a course in self-understanding, or perhaps he brought himself under some physical and psychological disciplines. He may have found a good counselor. They had many counselors in Jesus' day; they didn't have offices, but they were easily available. People didn't call them "Doctor," they called them Grandma or Grandpa. Or maybe the man got a better job, or moved to a nicer neighborhood, so that life was measurably better. One way or another, the man was now *clean,* and it was wonderful.

Cleansing is one of the basic biblical terms for spiritual renewal. In the Old Testament people stopped at a laver of water and washed their hands to symbolize their quest for moral cleanliness. The priests of the Old Testament had quite structured practices of cleansing in connection with their work. Under particular circumstances there were also ritual patterns of cleansing for persons outside the priesthood. I've sometimes heard people speak of their faith experience as making them feel "so clean." The language is right. We think of evil conduct as being filthy; and when we change our ways, we feel we've been cleansed. So when we read that this man was free from his unclean spirit, we can sense the happiness he must have felt. Once he had been the site of an unclean spirit, but now he was clean.

Only one thing was wrong. He was *empty.* He was clean, but he was empty.

Meanwhile, Jesus said, the unclean spirit was wandering through "waterless regions looking for a resting place" (Matthew 12:43), but without success. But one day in the midst of his wanderings, he decided to visit the old neighborhood. As the spirit put it, "I will return to my house from which I came." Did you notice what the unclean spirit said: "I will return to *my* house." The spirit thinks he has a claim on this man's life, so he can refer to the man as "my house." The man may have felt it was enough to be cleaned, reformed, proper and nice. But as long as his life was unoccupied, as long as he was empty, it's as if there were a sign on his soul that said "Room for Rent. Immediate Occupancy."

That's apparently what the unclean spirit saw in this man. So when this spirit found the man's house "empty, swept, and put in order," it was just the sort of situation it was looking for. After all, what could be more challenging to an unclean spirit than a *clean, empty* house?

Indeed, it was such an exciting prospect that the unclean spirit couldn't keep the good fortune to itself. Even unclean spirits have a certain demonic generosity. So it went out, Jesus said, and got "seven other spirits more evil than itself," and they all moved into the man's life. Now, Jesus said, this man's condition was worse than it was at the first. Before he was cleaned up, the man was indwelt by just one unclean spirit; but as the story ends, he is inhabited by eight, with seven of them worse than the original tenant. It's a very sad story, and an unpleasant one; to think that someone was delivered from the uncleanness of life only to end up not only back in his old, troubled ways but worse off than before. Seven times worse off, in fact.

Why was Jesus telling this story to these good people? True, they were Jesus' enemies, but they were not bad people. They were "clean" people. Whatever moral filth had once marked their lives, it was no longer there. So how did Jesus' story apply to these good people?

And that, you see, is the very point of the story. This is a parable of what can happen to *good* people; specifically, to good, *empty* people. Or to turn to some of our contemporary expectations, this is a parable about what it means to have found "the good life," but still be empty.

You don't have to be a professional theologian to understand this story. Many years ago an alcoholic in Green Bay, Wisconsin, helped me understand it. He was a dedicated member of Alcoholics Anonymous and a vibrant Christian, Lutheran by particular denomination and Christian by anyone's standard. He had high regard for the work done by Alcoholics Anonymous; after all, their program had been his way of deliverance from a way of life that had been destroying him. But he impressed upon me that too many members of AA stop too soon. Too many, he said, were satisfied if they could only stop drinking. As a result, as he put it, "they went from being wet alcoholics to being dry alcoholics." In truth, he put it more vividly than that, but if I quoted him exactly you would forget everything else I'm saying and would remember only his colorful language. But his point was center target: If a person gets swept clean of alcohol addiction but doesn't get something to fill his or her life, the thing in that person that led to alcoholism will now find a distorted expression somewhere else. That's the danger of being good and empty.

I preach in a wide variety of churches all around the country. In almost every instance I get the uneasy feeling that I am looking out on many good, empty people. Not all of them come under this category, of course, but a painful number seem to have gotten just good enough to be miserable. In so many faces there is no sign of the Christian quality of joy, and perhaps not a lot of love. They frown their way through an hour of the wonder of communing with Almighty God. They seem to be persons who probably never do anything very wrong, but who have limited joy, and who probably bring little joy to the world around them. They seem to be rather well cleaned, but painfully empty.

The people to whom I preach are mostly Protestants, but Roman Catholicism wrestles with the same problem. Roughly half a century ago, Father Ronald Knox was one of the most articulate priests in England. He said that probably it was perfectly possible to get to heaven by being "negatively good," by which he meant being attentive to the Ten Commandments, going to Mass fairly regularly, and "designing your whole life so that it shall be a scolding for other people." But then Father Knox raised a question: "I wonder how many people *really* get to heaven like that?" He insisted that there had to be more: real love for God, real love for neighbor, and not just a cold and proper regard for a neighbor's rights. Knox feared that many Catholics were superficially good, while inside they were empty.

What is true of the world of organized religion is even more dramatically true of our culture as a whole. Gregg Easterbrook, author of *The Progress Paradox: How Life Gets Better While People Feel Worse,* notes that by "practically every objective measure, American life has been getting better for decades." He notes that our typical house is more than twice as large as a generation ago, that more Americans graduate from college every year, that life expectancy keeps rising, and that almost all forms of disease are in decline. Crime has dropped "spectacularly," and most pollution is in decline. Yet with all these good signs, "the percentage of Americans who describe themselves as happy has not increased since the early 1950's, while incidence of depression keeps rising" (Gregg Easterbrook, "Progress Paradox," *Lexington [Ky.] Herald-Leader,* 3-14-04, D-1).

What is true of our American society in general (and probably the society of western Europe as well) may be even more dramatically true of the generation of youth and young adults. Dr. David Myers, professor of psychology at Hope College, says that today's youth and young adults "have grown up with much more affluence, slightly less overall happiness, much greater risk of depression, and a tripled teen suicide rate. Never has a culture experienced such physical comfort combined with such psychological misery. Never have we felt so free or had our prisons so overstuffed. Never have we been so sophisticated about pleasure or so likely to suffer broken relationships" (*The Christian Century,* 2-8-03, Vol. 120, No. 3, page 28).

All of this defies logic, doesn't it?—that we should have so many things we've wanted, then find so little satisfaction in them. Does it seem to you (as it does to me) that the analyses of our culture given by Dr. Easterbrook and Dr. Myers sound somehow reminiscent of the man in Jesus' story? Here we are, a people whose lives are swept clean, blessed with increased life expectancy, in possession of car and computer, and hooked up with the Internet—but so many strangely *empty.* Then, when the changing fortunes of life sweep over us, an unclean spirit looks in and says, "What a lovely place! The hedges trimmed, the welcome mat out, and empty!"

I think of T. S. Eliot, the premier poet many would say, of

the early and mid-twentieth century, who described the people of his time as "hollow men, their heads stuffed with straw" ("The Hollow Men"). His description seems more apt today than when he wrote it. And perhaps the particular tragedy of our time is that so many who are hollow—clean, but empty—don't see their state for what it is because they've stuffed their lives with straw. We've found the good life, but it doesn't satisfy as we thought it would. And there's no straw stuffing that takes the place of reality.

But let me come back to home base. As concerned as I am with our culture in general, I'm particularly concerned with you and me—we folks who are church members at least, and Christians at best. Jesus wasn't really talking to the culture in general, he was talking to people like us: "good" people, who are clean, who mostly do the right thing. Because we're crucial to the human story. I don't mean to be presumptuous, but the future of the human race depends strategically on the *good* people. We're the ones who are supposed to make a difference in the whole human picture. So what about us?

Well, we're in danger of being like the man in Jesus' parable. We too easily settle for being clean, good, and nice, because this is more or less in our control. On the surface, this is something we can bring off. We can reform, making ourselves a little bit better. We can discipline ourselves to the point where we become rather admirable. But we can't *fill* ourselves. We can occupy ourselves, by keeping busy, even to the point of nervous exhaustion. But we can't fill ourselves. Having gotten all tidied up, we're still empty. The filling has to come from outside ourselves. This is God's doing, and God alone can bring it off.

So Jesus kept directing people to a better way. I have come, he said, that you might have *life*. Not just a clean house, admirable as this is, but life. And still more. Jesus said not only that he had come that we might have life, but that we might "have it abundantly" (John 10:10). This is the kind of life that overflows. It is clean, of course, but more important, it is also full. So full that as you pass by it, you are caught by the excitement of its abundance. When I see people like that, I understand what the Christian life is meant to be.

The culture in which we currently live is, in its secular way, a rather clean, empty house. Not morally clean, but as clean as secularity can make it. With our scientific progress, our social reform, and our earnest ambition, we have made available to millions comforts and excitements that kings of other generations couldn't have dreamed of. But we're still left with so many empty houses, even among some of the most exemplary people. It seems that every time we find a new political, economic, or social gain, seven worse devils come with it.

Our world has enough people who are good and empty. We need a magnificent core of *full* people. Not just nice people or good people, much as I appreciate such; not even just saved people. Our culture needs *full* people, persons whose lives are a grand and holy passion, who are living so abundantly that in their presence you feel the overflow. This kind of fullness comes from a consistent walk with God, and it is within the reach of every one of us. It may not be easy, but neither is it terribly complicated. It just awaits our accepting God's way and doing it. Care to give it a try?

CHAPTER 6

Risky Business

MATTHEW 13:45-46: Again, the kingdom of heaven is like a merchant in search of fine pearls; on finding one pearl of great value, he went and sold all that he had and bought it.

Artists around the world have been inclined to portray Jesus with the complexion and the facial contours of their own people. I suspect this is an unconscious tribute to our Lord; it is our way of saying that we feel he belongs to us, whoever or wherever we may be. In the same way, our passing generations view Jesus and his teachings through the lens of our cultures. Our contemporary generation, with our sometimes-exalted opinion of our achievements, is particularly disposed toward making Jesus as modern or postmodern as possible.

Take the matter of Jesus' sales appeal. We may not immediately picture Jesus as "selling" something, but surely that's what he was about. He was announcing God's coming kingdom, and he was trying to enlist followers to promote the Kingdom. But when you look critically at his approach, you have to confess that he wasn't very sensitive to the rules of sales psychology. At least, not the kind of sales psychology we practice in the twenty-first-century world. And that includes the world of religious sales, at least as we see it generally practiced. Apparently Jesus didn't have a clue about how to attract people; or if he did, he didn't seem to care.

For example, see how he embarked on his ministry. The Gospels of both Matthew and Mark tell us that Jesus began with the message, "Repent, for the kingdom of heaven has come near" (Matthew 4:17). *Repent* isn't the ideal opening word. It isn't customer friendly. It's not good sales psychology. The aim is to get people hooked, then very slowly and artfully, and maybe even half deceptively, you tell them the price. Sometimes you don't even tell the full price. You say something like, "It's only $28 a month," and you don't mention how many months, nor what the carrying charges will be. But it seems Jesus didn't understand this sort of thing. He began his pitch with the price, and an ugly price at that: *Repent!*

You may want to remind me that Jesus was offering an especially appealing product, namely, a Kingdom. That's a very big deal, so perhaps under those circumstances you can be forthright about the price. If that's your reasoning, I admit you have a point. And particularly as far as Jesus' primary audience, the Jews, were concerned. They had to be thrilled to hear about the kingdom of God, or the kingdom of heaven, because they had been under the heel of one foreign power or another for roughly six centuries. So when Jesus said that the Kingdom was very near, it had to be very big, very good news.

But no doubt people began soon to ask for particulars. That's the way the political process usually works. After a new and glamorous leader appears on the scene, we want to see a white paper, some basics of a political platform. I think it was that way with Jesus. I can hear people saying, "Teacher, what exactly do you have in mind with your 'Kingdom' talk?"

So Jesus did what he almost always did; he threw out a parable. "The kingdom of heaven is like a merchant in search of fine pearls." Any adult in the audience knew what he was talking about, and even a child could get the "pearl" reference. The pearl was a particularly cherished jewel, both for its economic value and for its innate beauty. Connoisseurs traveled the bazaars of the ancient world to find pearls of exquisite beauty. They came to know the difference between average and superb, between good and perfect.

Jesus describes such a person. He's a merchant, so he knows the territory. Others may look at a pearl and say, "Beautiful!" The merchant whispers to himself, "Very average." This man is looking for the truly magnificent, perhaps one of a kind. He wants a pearl that will make ordinary people gasp, but which will make the most knowing faint away. So month after month, year after year, as he goes about his ordinary business, he continues his passionate search. Sometimes he almost forgets his sustaining work in order to track down one more lead toward the prize of his life. Through one country after another, sometimes in fashionable shops and sometimes in offbeat places, he keeps looking because one never knows where the truly superior might be found.

Then one day he comes upon it. He senses at a glance that this is it; but he must be sure, so he examines it over and over. I think he even leaves the shop for a time, reasoning with himself that he may be so intoxicated with his dreams that he's likely to project grandeur where it doesn't really exist. But when he returns to the shop, he knows beyond doubt that this pearl is the one he has been seeking. When he hears the price, great as it is, he doesn't even try to negotiate. He knows the pearl is worth everything the dealer asks. Indeed, for this man who has been seeking just such perfection, the pearl is worth more than the asking price. He must have it!

Now he calculates his resources. Obviously his cash on hand won't be enough. Nor does he have enough in his savings. He will have to sell the other pearls and jewels he owns. Yes, and more than that. He will have to sell his business, into which he has poured his energy for so many years. Still more. He will have to sell his home. He will have to dispose of everything in his possession. *Everything!*—just to get this pearl.

So he asks the dealer to hold it for him. He leaves all of the cash with the man, as an earnest payment, a mark of good faith, and promises to be back in a set number of days with the rest of the price. And he rushes home to sell everything, everything, everything, to get that pearl.

The people in Jesus' crowd are caught up with the wild excitement of the story. But now I hear a sturdy farmer say to the storekeeper from his town, "Any man who'd do that would be a fool. A blundering fool."

And Jesus says, "That's what the kingdom of heaven is like. It's like that pearl. You sell everything you have in order to get it." And I'm very sure I hear some in the crowd whisper, "Not I. This kingdom of heaven isn't for me, if that's the price."

You see what I mean? Jesus didn't know how to appeal to people. He didn't put his product in reach. He didn't tell them all the benefits of the pearl, didn't let them know why someone should pay such a price, didn't try to prove the Kingdom is worth it. He didn't even bother to describe the pearl's beauty, to suggest the deal was worth considering. Instead, he offered them this risky business: Sell everything, all you have accumulated and all that means so much to you, on a venture of love.

So it seems we know better today how to reach people. We don't talk much about the price of the Kingdom, and we don't emphasize the risk. We promise people heaven and an escape from hell. We tell them that this is the way to be happy, and perhaps we even suggest that this is the road to success. It's a wonderful way to live. And to be honest with you, I've found it to be so. When I was eighteen years old, I traveled one summer with a male quartet. Each evening, in one town after another, we would begin our program with our theme song, "Oh, I'm Satisfied with Jesus in My Heart." We sang it, and we meant it.

And I want to tell you that it's been true for me. I've been satisfied with Jesus. One hundred percent. But of course I don't live in the Sudan, where my wife or children or I myself might be sold into slavery for following Christ. And I don't live in North Korea, where my life would be in danger for believing as I do. Nor do I live in other countries, where if I told my neighbor about Christ, I would be thrown in prison, brought to trial, perhaps even executed.

On the other hand, I have to say that those preachers who told me about Christ were pretty candid about the possibilities. The days of my childhood were the days of the Great Depression. People were accustomed to looking life squarely in the eye. If you could look at your landlord without blinking, you could handle the preacher and the sermon too. I was only ten years old when I made the decision to follow Christ, but the sermons I heard made it clear that my decision might be costly. It was the only way to live, they said, but it comes at a price. They explained that I might lose some of my friends, that I might become unpopular, that I'd probably never get rich, and that there'd be some jobs I couldn't take because they would violate my convictions. Sometimes they would speak about God's call. I got the impression I might be sent to some mission field where I'd be scared to death, and that I'd probably die there, never seeing my folks and my home state of Iowa again. Those good old preachers made clear that the gospel was risky business. When I went down the aisle that night, and all the other times when I rededicated myself (as I did some hundreds of times), I knew that this kingdom of God was risky business.

Later I contemplated the risk at other levels. I came to an age when I wanted some proofs to support my purchase of this pearl. How did I know that Jesus Christ was my Savior? Because I had experienced his power in my life. But now the interrogator said, "But any good psychology book can explain that." And then there was the Bible. I placed so much store by it, read it every day, read it through every year, memorized its verses, found my innocent humor in its pages. But the interrogator asked how I could be sure it was true. I found all kinds of impressive data to support my love of the Scriptures. But I came slowly to realize that Søren Kierkegaard was right: You can take the evidence to a certain point, but then you have to take a risk. At the end of all the proof, you have to take the "leap of faith." The data, the logic, the experiences, the proof go only so far, and then you come to a place where you have to "faith it"; you have to take a leap out into God's trust.

So Jesus said, "The kingdom of heaven is like a merchant who found a pearl of great price. He sold everything. Everything! And he bought the pearl." And Jesus stopped right there. The inference is clear. If you want to get into this Kingdom business, you'll have to sell everything and gamble it on that pearl.

But we don't often tell the story that way today. We're more psychologically astute. We say, "Isn't our church nursery lovely—well equipped and nurturing? And have you heard about our youth program? It's one of the best. And our music: Don't you like our music? If you don't, we'll change it."

Now take a deep breath. Tell them about the cross. Because our Kingdom message says that if you follow Jesus, you have to take up a cross. Every day.

And someone says, "This sounds like risky business, this cross you're talking about." And if we're honest, we answer, "It is. But look at the Pearl. There's nothing like it. It's worth the risk."

Now the person to whom we're talking turns thoughtful, maybe even just a bit belligerent. "How dare anyone ask me to take such a risk? Who has a right to ask such a thing of me or of anyone else?"

Only Someone who knows the ultimate about risks. Only Someone who could say, "I have just one Son. I will send him to a cross on the gamble that if I do, some of you will take your risk in return. I'm going to risk my only Son on a world of self-centered, self-satisfied, self-seeking human beings, on the chance that some of them will bet their lives in return. Because I know that these humans have the potential to be eternity-centered, and to give grandly of all that they are. So I've taken a risk on them because I know they're worth it."

Jesus said that it's a pearl of great price. But you'll have to sell out to get it. It's a huge risk. Still, it doesn't seem too much to ask, since God risked Everything to extend the offer.

And as for me, I'm still satisfied. After all these years, I'm still satisfied. And there's still heaven to come.

CHAPTER 7

Miracles Can Be Overrated

LUKE 16:19-31: "There was a rich man who was dressed in purple and fine linen and who feasted sumptuously every day. And at his gate lay a poor man named Lazarus, covered with sores, who longed to satisfy his hunger with what fell from the rich man's table; even the dogs would come and lick his sores. The poor man died and was carried away by the angels to be with Abraham. The rich man also died and was buried. In Hades, where he was being tormented, he looked up and saw Abraham far away with Lazarus by his side. He called out, 'Father Abraham, have mercy on me, and send Lazarus to dip the tip of his finger in water and cool my tongue; for I am in agony in these flames.' But Abraham said, 'Child, remember that during your lifetime you received your good things, and Lazarus in like manner evil things; but now he is comforted here, and you are in agony. Besides all this, between you and us a great chasm has been fixed, so that those who might want to pass from here to you cannot do so, and no one can cross from there to us.' He said, 'Then, father, I beg you to send him to my father's house—for I have five brothers—that he may warn them, so that they will not also come into this place of torment.' Abraham replied, 'They have Moses and the prophets; they should listen to them.' He said, 'No, father Abraham; but if someone goes to them from the dead, they will repent.' He said to him, 'If they do not listen to Moses and the prophets, neither will they be convinced even if someone rises from the dead.' "

We humans have always been miracle seekers. Sometimes it's because of our need, as when we pray for a healing of the incurable or when we hope for what seems to be the impossible. But perhaps it's more a matter of proportion. We want something out of the ordinary. Even that which is loveliest, most astounding, and most beautiful can become commonplace if it is our daily fare. The great seventeenth-century poet and preacher John Donne told his London congregation one Easter Sunday that there is nothing God has established in our constant course of nature (which is therefore part of every day) that wouldn't seem a miracle if it were done but once. I suspect that if the sun rose only once in one's lifetime, we would wait all our days for that one inestimable miracle.

Especially, we want miracles that will substantiate our faith. I wonder how many times over the years someone has said to me, "If only I could see a miracle! It would mean so much to my faith if only once, just once, I could see something that was really miraculous."

Jesus told a story one day about two men. One had everything, and the other had nothing. Jesus was telling the story for the particular benefit of some Pharisees, "who were lovers of money" (Luke 16:14). The rich man was "dressed in purple and fine linen," which is to say that he got his wardrobe at the most exclusive haberdashery. It may even be that he had his own private tailor. That sort of thing happened in the first-century world of slavery, where captives brought from conquered countries were often skilled in crafts or even trained in a profession. Still more, he "feasted sumptuously every day" (Luke 16:19). The late William Barclay said that the Greek word that was used for this refers to eating that is gluttonous as well as exotic and costly.

"Well," someone says, "he earned the money; he had a right to it." Perhaps. Or perhaps he inherited it. But really, it doesn't matter whether he earned it or inherited it or was just extraordinarily fortunate in his financial dealings; the compelling issue has to do with how he used the wealth once he had it. It's clear that he was providing well for himself, but right at his gate lay "a poor man named Lazarus, covered with sores." He was so poor, in fact, that he hoped simply "to satisfy his hunger with what fell from the rich man's table" (Luke 16:21).

In that ancient Middle Eastern culture, the dining area for a fine home was likely to be out-of-doors—*alfresco,* thank you. Passersby or even beggars were therefore often close at hand. In a world without eating utensils or napkins, people ate with their hands, and when they wanted to remove grease or dressing from their hands they wiped them on a piece of bread, then threw the bread to the ground or to anyone who might be standing nearby—much the way someone eating in a downtown city park throws scraps to the pigeons. It seems that Lazarus kept himself alive by just such scraps. As for his sores, the dogs came and licked them. We may see that action as a redeeming kindness in this poor man's life; though in a culture where dogs were generally seen as scavenger animals, the inference may be quite otherwise.

Well, in time both men died. Death is, indeed, the great equalizer. Eventually everyone takes this journey. The wealthy may be able to postpone it longer, but no one postpones it forever. Lazarus died first, and he went in style! He was "carried away by the angels to be with Abraham" (Luke 16:22). One of our African American spirituals has such a line for death: "a band of angels, / coming after me, / coming for to carry me home" ("Swing Low, Sweet Chariot"). I suspect the unknown writer of the spiritual may have gotten the phrase from Luke's Gospel, feeling his or her kinship with Lazarus.

The rich man didn't fare so well. Jesus' words are painfully succinct: he "died and was buried," and the next thing we know he is "in Hades," a place of torment (Luke 16:22-23).

Now that we see these two men in their destinations, something else might occur to us. Jesus refers to the beggar by name, Lazarus (a name which, by the way, means "God is my help"), but he doesn't give us a name for the rich man. Scholars eventually called him *Dives,* which is Latin for *rich,* but Jesus makes him anonymous. I wonder if perhaps our Lord is suggesting that in the eternal records, Lazarus is better known than the rich man? At the very least, Jesus is having fun with our usual standards of evaluation. The rich and powerful in our world have names in the sports, entertainment, business, and society sections of the newspaper, while vast numbers never find a line in the press, unless they live in one of those wonderful little communities with an all-encompassing weekly paper. But God's standards are different from ours. Lazarus gets more mention than what's-his-name, the rich man.

The rich man's destination isn't very nice. No purple and linen there, no sumptuous eating, no servants to fan one when the heat is excessive. But there is a good view, although an upsetting one. He can see where Lazarus is, in Abraham's care—"in his bosom," as the full translation puts it. This was a uniquely Jewish way of picturing heaven; the blessed are in the embrace of their most cherished ancestor. The rich man remembers Lazarus's name, which is an interesting detail, since obviously he never worried about him when he begged outside his gate. Now he appeals to Abraham to send Lazarus to dip a finger in water to put a cooling drop on his tongue. If I may say so, I think the rich man is still suffering from the servant syndrome; he feels he can still expect someone to attend to his needs. Apparently old habits and attitudes die slowly, even in Hades.

Abraham responds kindly to the rich man's plea, calling him "Child." But he reminds the rich man that in his lifetime he had received good things and Lazarus evil things, but that now Lazarus is comforted while he is in agony. A point is implicit in Abraham's response: Rich man, did you worry yourself about Lazarus's needs when you saw his misery over the years? As for the request for help from Lazarus, Abraham replied, "Between you and us a great chasm has been fixed" (Luke 16:26). Again, a point is implicit: There was no gulf when Lazarus needed relief; why didn't you extend some help when it was so easy to do so?

If the world is divided between the Haves—the rich man—and the Have-nots—Lazarus—this is a painful story for all of us who belong to the Haves. And the odds are great that most of us who are reading this book belong to the Haves. To begin with, we're among those who can read, in a world where an estimated one billion adults cannot. To be able to read is decidedly a "Have" position, and as a lover of books and periodicals I cherish it. And most if not all of us who at this moment are thinking together in this book will get three meals today if we want them, and perhaps a snack or two along the way. A fair percentage of us worry about our weight; and when we record our weight for our driver's license, we generally enter a figure we're aiming for rather than the one the scales currently report. We may not be multimillionaires, but most of us are classified among the world's Haves.

I'm uncomfortable about this when I read Jesus' report of the conversation between Abraham and the rich man. (Perhaps I should add, "the rich man who is no longer very rich.") In a world where there are Haves and Have-nots, God apparently looks quite critically on the Haves. He doesn't mind our having; indeed, God seems pleased to bless us with abundance; our universe overflows with benefits, from the resources within its bowels to the planets around us. But God expects us to treat these resources as a sacred responsibility, especially as long as some Have-nots exist.

Dorothy Sayers is still best known around the world for her detective novels, built around the fictional Lord Peter Wimsey; but Sayers was also a challenging lay theologian. In one of her essays she noted that the church has always had organizations to deal with sexual immorality; why don't we also have some to deal with financial immorality? She asks, "Do the officials stationed at church doors in Italy to exclude women with bare arms turn anybody away on the grounds that they are too well-dressed to be honest?" Since there are vigilance committees that are concerned for morally suggestive books and plays, she says, ought there not also to be vigilance committees to deal with "literature which 'suggests' that getting on in the world is the chief object in life?" But then Ms. Sayers reminds us that the church is not the Vatican or the Bench of Bishops; "the Church is you and I" (Dorothy L. Sayers, *Creed or Chaos?* [Manchester, N.H.: Sophia Institute Press, 1999], page 136). As I sit thinking about Lazarus and the rich man, Ms. Sayers's questions make me worry about what I have. I used to worry about what I had not; now I worry more about what I have, and what I am doing with it.

But there's still more to this story. I suggested at the outset that we are lovers of miracles, and that perhaps miracles are overrated. This rich man now appeals for a miracle. He appeals to Abraham, "I beg you to send [Lazarus] to my father's house—for I have five brothers—that he may warn them, so that they will not also come into this place of torment" (Luke 16:27-28). At first thought, this appeal makes one think better of the rich man. He is concerned about somebody else. But he limits his concern rather exclusively: Send someone to help my brothers. If this place to which the rich man has been consigned is so bad, he should want to spare everyone from coming here. I wish the rich man had a broader vision of human need.

But more than that, I wish he would express some remorse for the kind of conduct that got him where he is; I wish he would acknowledge that he mistreated Lazarus and that he used his wealth badly. I see no evidence of soul-searching. I'm no authority on the world to come, and I don't really want to know too much about hell. It seems to me, however, that one would hope hell would make persons evaluate their lives; that they would ponder why it is that they've gotten to such a state. As far as this story is concerned, we might conclude that such redeeming thoughts don't occur to hell's occupants. This may be a rather instructive point.

In any event, hear Abraham's answer, as Jesus reports it. "They have Moses and the prophets; they should listen to them." Now the rich man makes his argument for the miraculous. "No, father Abraham; but if someone goes to them from the dead, they will repent" (Luke 16:29-30). This seems a reasonable argument. I've heard similar contentions many times. I may sometimes have thought this way myself: If only I could see a miracle, I would never doubt again!

But hear Abraham's reply. "If they do not listen to Moses and the prophets, neither will they be convinced even if someone rises from the dead" (Luke 16:31). This contradicts our everyday assumption that if only we could see a miracle, we would believe. Not so, Jesus tells us; if we aren't convinced by "Moses and the prophets"—that is, the revealed Scriptures—we won't be convinced by miracles.

W. Russell Hindmarsh, one of England's eminent scientists in the mid-twentieth century, reminded us that the persuasiveness of any given miracle depends on the faith we bring to it. He pointed to the story of Israel. The Red Sea had opened for them as they fled from Egypt. The writer of Exodus noted that it had happened through a natural phenomenon, a "strong east wind" that blew all night (Exodus 14:21). The Israelites saw it as a miracle, as indeed it was, since the timeliness of the wind made their safe passage possible. But some time later, when they were in trouble, they wished they had never left Egypt! What happened to the miracle? How could they forget such a marvelous event? Professor Hindmarsh said that it was "the accepting by the Hebrews of this natural event, in faith, as the work of God on their behalf which constitutes it as a miracle" (*Proceedings of the Eleventh World Methodist Conference,* Lee F. Tuttle and Max W. Woodward, editors [London: The Epworth Press, 1967], page 131). When Israel's faith was gone, the miracle went with it.

Miracles, so to speak, come and go. If we observe an event by faith, we see the miracle that is there. But if we approach the same event with unbelief, we will find a way to explain the miracle. So suppose Lazarus or someone else had been raised from the dead and had come to the rich man's brothers, would they have been converted? For a while, perhaps; for as long as the event impressed them. But when they came to a time when for reasons of their own they found it more convenient to think otherwise, they would find a way around the miracle.

Consider, then, what Jesus was saying about the Scriptures. Obviously, he considered them far more important than miracles. No wonder, then, that when Jesus walked with two disciples late on the first Easter, "he interpreted to them the things about himself in all the scriptures," "beginning with Moses and all the prophets" (Luke 24:27). I suspect Jesus understood very well that there might come a time when the disciples would doubt the inestimable miracle of the Resurrection; at such a time, they would need the abiding witness of the Scriptures.

Because our Bibles are so near at hand, so easily in arm's reach, we discount their calm, strong witness of love, of reason, of faith and hope and truth. Miracles are nice. I'm glad for some I've observed. But the Scriptures are better. Jesus said so.

CHAPTER 8

Second Chance for a Poor Manager

LUKE 16:1-13: Then Jesus said to the disciples, "There was a rich man who had a manager, and charges were brought to him that this man was squandering his property. So he summoned him and said to him, 'What is this that I hear about you? Give me an account of your management, because you cannot be my manager any longer.' Then the manager said to himself, 'What will I do, now that my master is taking the position away from me? I am not strong enough to dig, and I am ashamed to beg. I have decided what to do so that, when I am dismissed as manager, people may welcome me into their homes.' So, summoning his master's debtors one by one, he asked the first, 'How much do you owe my master?' He answered, 'A hundred jugs of olive oil.' He said to him, 'Take your bill, sit down quickly, and make it fifty.' Then he asked another, 'And how much do you owe?' He replied, 'A hundred containers of wheat.' He said to him, 'Take your bill and make it eighty.' And his master commended the dishonest manager because he had acted shrewdly; for the children of this age are more shrewd in dealing with their own generation than are the children of light. And I tell you, make friends for yourselves by means of dishonest wealth so that when it is gone, they may welcome you into the eternal homes.

"Whoever is faithful in a very little is faithful also in much; and whoever is dishonest in a very little is dishonest also in much. If then you have not been faithful with the dishonest wealth, who will entrust to you the true riches? And if you have not been faithful with what belongs to another, who will give you what is your own? No slave can serve two masters; for a slave will either hate the one and love the other, or be devoted to the one and despise the other. You cannot serve God and wealth."

I overheard a conversation recently that you probably heard too. Not the same conversation, obviously, but one so much like it that you'll nod your head in recognition as soon as I quote it. The woman in the adjoining restaurant booth was upset by discourteous service. The man—her husband, I think—answered, "You'd never guess that jobs are hard to get these days, would you? You'd think anyone who has a job would do their best to keep it." And the woman rejoined, "Well, you know from your own business that good workers are always hard to find."

And I said to myself, *God knows that better than anybody. God, the longest-term employer in our universe, knows how hard it is to get good, dependable workers.*

As I had this conversation with myself, I was thinking especially of myself. I'm one of those people who considers himself called by God to a special kind of work, so I'm particularly sensitive to God's executive problems. But I'm not being defensive when I say that I'm not the only employee who has given God a hard time.

Which leads us to a story Jesus told one day. Jesus left us with several strange stories, but this one may be the strangest of all. There was a certain rich man, Jesus said, who had a manager; and word came to the rich man that this manager was "squandering his property." Jesus doesn't say if the man was being intentionally fraudulent; I'm inclined to feel that he was simply incompetent. But whatever, it's a serious shortcoming when a manager squanders the resources that have been entrusted to him. After all, the purpose of a manager is to relieve the owner of worry. This fellow is failing in the very matter for which he has been hired.

The manner in which the rich man deals with the crisis sounds very much like our twenty-first-century world. Some things don't change that much. "What is this that I hear about you?" the rich man asks his manager. "Give me an accounting of your management, because you cannot be my manager any longer" (Luke 16:2). That is—"Clean out your desk and bring in your books, because this is your last week." It's a painful scene, but it appears the manager deserves to be let go.

But before the manager begins totaling his employer's books for a final report, he does some accounting of his own situation. In this he shows some wisdom. There are times when what we need most is to have a little talk with ourselves. The manager asked himself what he would do when he lost this job. "I am not strong enough to dig, and I am ashamed to beg" (Luke 16:3). It's a succinct and fascinating analysis. I get a feeling the man is inclined to be a bit easy on himself. I'm not sure he's not strong enough to dig, but I'm quite sure he's out of practice. It seems likely that he has treated himself tenderly for some time. But he still has a self-image that he can't give up; he just can't imagine himself a beggar.

Then suddenly, a moment of enlightenment. He comes up with a very clever scheme. It isn't an ethical one, but it's ingenious. He will go to some of his boss's debtors and will offer them a reduced amount for quick payment: "You owe for a hundred jugs of olive oil? Make it fifty." "You owe for a hundred containers of wheat? Make it eighty." I think that this can be interpreted two ways. It may be that the manager was working for his employer's good, in that he would get quicker payment by offering this discount. Or he may have been entirely fraudulent, falsifying accounts to save money for the debtors and in the process putting them in a position where he could blackmail them if he needed to do so. In either event, he would make friends of these debtors so that when he was unemployed, one of them might take him on.

However you read it, the manager is a bit of a scoundrel,

and you expect his employer to treat him accordingly. Instead, the employer praises him, "because he had acted shrewdly" (Luke 16:8)! Jesus goes on to comment that "the children of this age are more shrewd in dealing with their own generation than are the children of light" (Luke 16:8). As Jesus finished the story, he added a sermonette for his disciples. "Whoever is faithful in a very little is faithful also in much; and whoever is dishonest in a very little is dishonest also in much. If then you have not been faithful with the dishonest wealth, who will entrust to you the true riches? And if you have not been faithful with what belongs to another, who will give you what is your own?" (Luke 16:10-12).

It's a strange story. In a sense, there's no need for me to look for the "back side" of this parable, because the whole story seems to come to us from the back side. All the characters are on the shady side: the manager because he was a poor employee to begin with and went from there to being marginal in his ethics; the debtors because they happily cooperate with a questionable scheme; and the executive because he smiles benignly on the whole affair, even to the point of praising his manager's conduct.

Let me interrupt myself long enough to note that this isn't the only time Jesus used questionable characters and questionable situations in order to make a point in a parable. In his story of the man who found treasure in a field and sold everything to buy the field (Matthew 13:44), honorable ethics, it seems to me, would have compelled the man to reveal his secret information. Otherwise this man reminds me of someone who buys a piece of property for a bargain price when he learns that the highway commission is about to establish a new interchange at that spot. Or think of Jesus' parable about being persistent in prayer, when he tells of an unjust judge who "neither feared God nor had respect for people" (Luke 18:2), but who gave the persistent widow justice because he got tired of being pestered by her. Jesus was a very sophisticated storyteller. He introduced some characters and some situations for shock value. To be honest with you, Jesus didn't tell the sort of stories that we sometimes think of as Christian fiction, where it's very easy to tell who are the good guys and who are the bad guys. Jesus' stories, in their sophistication and character delineation, are right at home with the best Russian, English, and American novelists of the nineteenth, twentieth, and twenty-first centuries.

So what is Jesus telling us in this strange story in Luke 16:1-13? He certainly isn't giving business advice. He concludes the whole episode by warning us that we can't serve two masters: "You cannot serve God and wealth" (Luke 16:13). This is not a story about how to be a manager, a business owner, or a debtor; Jesus made that completely clear. In fact we're told that the Pharisees, "who were lovers of money," were offended by this parable, and that they ridiculed Jesus for telling it (see Luke 16:14).

Perhaps the Pharisees had good reason to be offended. It's quite possible that the parable was directed particularly at them. Mind you, it's a parable that is good for all of us; but in its first telling, the Pharisees may have been the primary audience, even though Jesus was speaking to his disciples. The Pharisees, after all, were the major managers of Judaism in the first century. They were the ones who considered themselves especially responsible for God's purposes in the world. And in truth, like the manager in the parable, they were "squandering" God's property. Jesus said, in another context, "For you cross sea and land to make a single convert, and you make the new convert twice as much a child of hell as yourselves" (Matthew 23:15). They were, indeed, abusing God's property, the property that had been entrusted to them.

But let's leave the Pharisees and talk about us, and what this parable might be saying to us. Almost surely the "rich man" represents God. God is surely the richest landowner we know. And God has subcontracted all his riches to managers. You, I, the person down the street, the entrepreneur, the entertainer, the athlete, the fellow living under the bridge, the teacher, the farmer—we're the managers. Whether we know it or not, and whether we realize we're under contract, we're the managers. We make the decisions about our universe and its resources, and about ourselves and our individual resources—our time, our abilities, our money, and our personalities. We're the managers.

The manager in the parable "was squandering" his master's property. One translation says the manager was "dissipating" the property, while some others use the word "wasting." In any event, I don't get the impression that the manager was actually defrauding his employer; rather, he seemed simply to be careless and incompetent. And he seemed to be getting by with it. Some commentators suggest that the owner probably lived a distance away, so there was little hands-on contact with the business; the whole project was left to the manager's discretion, and he had been indifferent.

Now his carelessness had caught up with him. Someone, we don't know who, brought charges against the manager. It was a wake-up call, but it looked as if it were too late. The office of management was being taken from him.

But all was not lost. Perhaps for the first time in a very long time, the manager did an inventory on his own conduct. Driven to the wall of reality, he showed some aptitude—perhaps the very aptitude that had caused the owner to hire him in the first place. He began to treat the property as if it were his own. What could he do with all these overdue accounts? By discounting them, he could perhaps bring some capital to his master, and he could certainly bring some benefit to himself. He was seeking creatively to make things happen, which is the way he should have treated his stewardship all along.

And the master is pleased. He doesn't inquire into the manager's motives; he simply rejoices that the fellow has left his dissolute ways and is becoming productive. I think perhaps the owner may even have congratulated himself, saying, "Perhaps I wasn't in error when I put this fellow in charge. Maybe all he needed was a good wake-up call. Now perhaps he'll amount to something."

Jesus was giving a summons to better management. In his parable, the owner demanded that the manager "give an accounting" of his stewardship. I'm altogether certain that some day God will call all of us to give an accounting. I don't know the specifics, but I believe that such a principle is written into the very nature of our universe. God, whose sense of economy is so demanding that every fallen leaf and every normal animal refuse is used to replenish the earth's soil quality, is not one who will wink indifferently at squandering managers. God will ask, "What have you done with what I lent you?" At a large scale, the wonders of nature and the resources of our planet will call for an accounting. At a personal level, there will someday be some sort of accounting of what we have done with the intelligence, the personality, the physical attractiveness, the social winsomeness in our possession. Have we used these resources to bless others, in the name of God, or have we squandered them in building some petty kingdom for ourselves?

Jesus said, "The children of this age are more shrewd in dealing with their own generation than are the children of light" (Luke 16:8). Might God be observing some athletes who are training for the Olympics and say, "I wish some of my preachers would strive that passionately for record-breaking excellence"—that is, the children of this age are more shrewd in their pursuits than those who identify themselves as children of light. Or might God be thinking, while seeing an entrepreneur work feverishly to get a better idea than her competitor, "Why don't my Sunday school teachers get that feverish in competing for the souls of their students?" Or again, might God wish, while seeing a sales representative go tirelessly from one prospect to another, that we were that dogged in our pursuit of wandering souls?

The manager in the parable was incompetent in the way he did his work; and when he was frightened into action, he followed a course that was questionable from an ethical point of view. But this you had to say for him: When he saw he was in trouble, he woke up. It wasn't pretty, but even a person who stumbles into the day is better than a slugabed.

As Luke reports it, this is a parable Jesus told as he was en route to Jerusalem. Beginning at that place in the story where Luke says that Jesus "set his face to go to Jerusalem" (Luke 9:51), there is an urgency in everything Jesus says and does—a kind of holy impatience. With the showdown only days away, Jesus knows that every hour counts. Very soon he will be betrayed and brought to trial. I think it is not by chance that so many of Jesus' parables during this final journey take on a particularly no-nonsense approach.

So it is that in this story I hear our Lord saying, "How is it that those who labor for filthy lucre go about their work with more imagination, more creativity, and more passion than those of you who are in the business of eternity? What in the name of heaven is wrong with my managers? And why are the children of this world wiser in their generation than the children of light?"

It's a wake-up call to us poor managers. Since we're still around, it looks as if we are getting another chance.

CHAPTER 9

A Laugh and a Prayer

LUKE 11:5-13; 18:1-8: And he said to them, "Suppose one of you has a friend, and you go to him at midnight and say to him, 'Friend, lend me three loaves of bread; for a friend of mine has arrived, and I have nothing to set before him.' And he answers from within, 'Do not bother me; the door has already been locked, and my children are with me in bed; I cannot get up and give you anything.' I tell you, even though he will not get up and give him anything because he is his friend, at least because of his persistence he will get up and give him whatever he needs.

"So I say to you, Ask, and it will be given to you; search, and you will find; knock, and the door will be opened for you. For everyone who asks receives, and everyone who searches finds, and for everyone who knocks, the door will be opened. Is there anyone among you who, if your child asks for a fish, will give a snake instead of a fish? Or if the child asks for an egg, will give a scorpion? If you then, who are evil, know how to give good gifts to your children, how much more will the heavenly Father give the Holy Spirit to those who ask him!"

Then Jesus told them a parable about their need to pray always and not to lose heart. He said, "In a certain city there was a judge who neither feared God nor had respect for people. In that city there was a widow who kept coming to him and saying, 'Grant me justice against my opponent.' For a while he refused; but later he said to himself, 'Though I have no fear of God and no respect for anyone, yet because this widow keeps bothering me, I will grant her justice, so that she may not wear me out by continually coming.'" And the Lord said, "Listen to what the unjust judge says. And will not God grant justice to his chosen ones who cry to him day and night? Will he delay long in helping them? I tell you, he will quickly grant justice to them. And yet, when the Son of Man comes, will he find faith on earth?"

During the first third of the twentieth century, one of America's favorite Bible teachers was a man named Rollin Walker. When I was the pastor of a church in Greater Cleveland many years later, some of my older members still delighted in recalling their college days in his classes at Ohio Wesleyan University. They remembered him, however, not only for his classroom skills but also for his prayers in the college chapel services, especially that he sometimes would pause in the midst of his prayers to laugh at something that he found amusing and that, no doubt, he felt God found amusing too.

The people who told me such stories cherished the memory. I suspect there were others who were offended at laughter coming in the midst of prayer. Personally, I like it. If prayer is an expression of our friendship with God, it ought surely to include more than appeals and repentance, and more even than the giving of thanks and the adoration of God. Prayer ought to have its moments of exuberance that burst into laughter. That's the mood of Psalm 126, which was written after Israel had returned from captivity. In verse 2 the writer says, "Then our mouth was filled with laughter." I like that.

But that isn't the only time when laughter is appropriate to prayer. Sometimes when I'm praying I have to smile at my own absurdity. Prayer is a particularly good time for being relieved of the burden of taking ourselves too seriously; in the process of such a down-sitting, one ought at least to chuckle if not laugh outright. One of my favorite saints is Teresa of Avila. She encouraged her nuns to dance in the cloister as an expression of their joy and to put castanets to use on feast-day celebrations, and she was inclined to carry on frank and amusing conversations with God. In one instance, unhappy with the style and manner of an abbess, Teresa complained to God, "Lord, if I had my way that woman wouldn't be Superior here"; and Teresa reported that God replied, "Teresa, if I had My way, she wouldn't be, either."

Yes, I believe there's a place for laughter in prayer. It's possible that the world would be a better place if more of us came smiling from the place of prayer. But there's one factor in prayer that isn't funny, and that's when our prayers are not being answered—or when the silence makes us conclude that the answer is no. When one prays days, weeks, or perhaps even months or years for what seems a quite reasonable request, and heaven seems coolly indifferent—it's hard to see the humor in such an experience.

It's no wonder, then, that we miss the laughter in two of Jesus' parables that have prayer as their theme, and unanswered prayer at that. We're inclined to read these parables with painful earnestness, because there's nothing amusing about unanswered prayers.

The first of these parables is reported to us by both Matthew and Luke. Suppose you have a friend, Jesus said, and you go to him at midnight because you have a predicament. An unexpected guest has come and you need to provide a hospitable snack, but you have "nothing to set before him" (Luke 11:6). Your neighbor has what you need, but he also has a sleeping family; and getting provisions for you will mean awakening the family, so the neighbor tries to send you on your way. It's important at this point to interrupt Jesus' story long enough to explain some differences between the first and the twenty-first centuries. For one, there were no 24/7 stores in those days, which, come to think of it, was also the case when I was a boy. Also, in that simple world all the family slept on mats on the floor, side by side. For the father to arise meant the likelihood of the whole family awakening, with the ensuing likelihood that the smaller children might cry for an extended period—and also, perhaps, a spouse might berate you for having such inconsiderate, middle-of-the-night neighbors. I discovered while traveling in the Middle East several years ago that the world of the Bible is for peasant families not that different from today. A Palestinian mother showed me her home: one room, with modest chairs for daytime use, and along one wall a stack of mats that were spread on the floor in the evening for the family beds.

The neighbor in Jesus' story is not a bad sort. He'd like to help out, but not at the price of disrupting his family. So in an insistent, vigorous whisper he tells his friend to go somewhere else with his problem. Now Jesus makes his point. Even though the man will not get up for his neighbor "because he is his friend, at least because of his persistence he will get up and give him whatever he needs" (Luke 11:8).

It's a funny story. I can imagine a contemporary screenwriter developing it for a television sitcom. Or perhaps for one of those artful commercials that manage to give us a complete scenario in twenty or thirty seconds. I can even imagine some of the particular actors I might use in such a television show; but since I want this book to be read for more than the next year or two, I won't offer those names lest I make the book dated for next year's readers. But I don't have to tell you that it's a funny story; or at least, I wouldn't have to tell you if you weren't so religious in your handling of the Bible that you miss a laugh even when it slapsticks itself on you.

The other parable, which appears only in Luke's Gospel, is funny in a different way; but I would still enjoy casting it with some contemporary performers. There was a judge in a certain city, Jesus said, "who neither feared God nor had respect for people" (Luke 18:2). He was a very unfeeling sort of man, and with a bit of a mean streak too. In this city there was also a widow. She had suffered a severe injustice, and there was little hope for her to get her rights. Widows didn't have much clout in the first-century world. She couldn't afford an attorney, and there was no Legal Aid Society to hear her appeal. Her only chance was this judge. If you're beginning to choose characters for this little drama, don't choose dramatic actors; get some with a comedic touch, because although it sounds as if we're dealing with pathos, it's not so. Bathos, rather, is going to be the mood.

Because this widow has one thing going for her: She's persistent. She keeps pestering the judge. He slips out of his home, and she's waiting on the corner. He approaches his office, and she's already at the door. He heads to his favorite social refuge, and she's there, smiling in a fashion that is maddening. He hates to admit that he is beaten, so he has to explain to himself why he's about to do what he is about to do: "Though I have no fear of God and no respect for anyone, yet because this widow keeps bothering me, I will grant her justice, so that she may not wear me out by continually coming" (Luke 18:4-5). The late William Barclay said that the judge's phrase that is here translated "wear me out" means literally, "lest she give me a black eye" (William Barclay, *The Gospel of Luke* [Philadelphia: The Westminster Press, 1956], page 231). Perhaps the judge feared the feisty woman would actually hit him in an unguarded moment; or perhaps he simply meant that if she caused him to lose any more sleep, he would soon have rings around his eyes. One way or another, he couldn't endure her any longer. So he gave her justice.

Again, it's a funny story, a delightful little burlesque on a serious problem. You don't need much imagination to picture a quite pompous judge who begins slipping around corners to avoid a quite powerless woman in widow's garb who is staking him out as if she were a private detective on his trail. When she wins, you not only cheer, you laugh, and laugh hard.

That brings us back to my point. Jesus is dealing with the same problem in these two parables, and it's a serious problem. Sometimes, in fact, it's heartbreaking. If you're praying for someone with a life-threatening malignancy, or if you've tried for years by both prayers and deeds to save a marriage, unanswered prayer is not a theological problem for thoughtful discussion; it is pain and disillusionment staring you in the face.

And in truth, there are no easy answers to this problem. J. B. Phillips, who blessed a generation of the English-speaking world with his translation of the New Testament, told of an experience at St. John's Church in Redhill, England. A man with inoperable cancer for whom he prayed was miraculously healed, while another man in the parish—a particularly godly man—received no healing of his cancer, though he was prayed for earnestly and at length. How come? Some quickly sweep such an issue under a sort of ecclesiastical carpet with the phrase, "It must be a question of God's will." That's an easy answer; and like so many easy answers, it's a bit of a cop-out. A very great deal of what happens in our world is not God's will; that's why Jesus taught us to pray, "Thy will be done, on earth as it is in heaven." We pray for God's will to be done because it won't automatically happen. God's will happens as God's people work, love, give, and pray to make it happen.

Which is to say, there's something at work in this world of ours that doesn't want God's will to happen. Sometimes it's obvious. When you pour your energy and prayer into opposing a pornographic store, you know well enough that someone else is pouring their energy into establishing such a store; when we pray for persecuted Christians in certain countries, we know there are powers in the government or in some institution that are working vigorously to wipe out the Christians. It's relatively easy in such instances to see the battle between God's will and the will of those who have a contrary agenda of their own.

But what do we say about those unanswered prayers

where the issues are not clearly drawn and where there is no visible enemy? What of the illness that strikes a loved one irrationally? What of the instances where we are victimized by an accident out of the blue or a freakish twist of nature that destroys a house and a family's lifetime mementos? What if I have prayed earnestly for the well-being of that loved one or have often pleaded with God to protect our household? What then?

Jesus answers with a funny story. Two of them, in fact. The one is a silly little predicament. The man with the midnight visitor will be embarrassed if he doesn't get some food, but he'll survive. A failure of hospitality is a significantly serious matter in the code of the Middle East, but it's not quite life and death. The widow's story, on the other hand, is deadly serious. If she doesn't get justice, it's quite likely her life soon would be reduced to begging in the streets. But in both cases, Jesus tells a story with a twinkle in his eye.

I tell you the truth: Some matters are too serious to be dealt with seriously. The Jewish people, who have suffered centuries of prejudice and persecution, have become famous for their sense of humor. Bill Adler says, in an introduction to a book on Jewish humor, that "in drama, tragedy celebrates man's passionate propensity to struggle and to die, whereas comedy celebrates his ability to endure and to survive" (Bill Adler, *Jewish Wit and Wisdom* [New York: Dell Publishing, 1969], page 8). In my years as a pastor, I often saw this quality in people who were undergoing great loss or pain; they insisted on laughing with me or on finding humor in their difficult state.

So is Jesus simply teaching us to have the typical stiff upper lip? Not at all. He's telling us that we live in a world where good doesn't necessarily win today, but where it will in the long run. And because we know this is so, we can smile even when we're confronted by the apparently inexplicable.

We are certain of several things. For one, that God is on

our side. God's answer may be "No," because what we ask for may be shortsighted or even destructive; most of us have looked back on prayers that were better answered in the negative! In other instances, God's answer is "Wait"; our view of time is time-bound and marked by the childish impatience of those who don't know all that is at stake. There is a time and a tide in the affairs of this life. What we ask for may be right, but not just now. And then there are those instances where, in our struggle for good—whether by prayer or by deeds or by both—we have simply come up against great opposition. I'm not surprised that this is so. I recognize that great evil exists in our world, and that many factors work as earnestly on behalf of evil as do the saints on behalf of good. When, like the neighbor in the parable, I keep knocking at the door, or like the widow in the other parable, I keep pestering the judge, I do so with a kind of holy audacity. I know God is on the side of the right. Mind you, my perception of the right is limited, but I intend to line up with God's will as much as I perceive it.

Devout Catholics refer to Saint Jude as the patron saint of lost causes. I have no such saint, but I engage in a good deal of praying that involves something of the same mindset. So I don't intend to quit praying, or for that matter, to quit working for the right. Listen to Jesus: If heaven seems silent, just keep knocking. And smile while you do so. God and the universe are on your side.

CHAPTER 10

It Happens While We Sleep

MATTHEW 13:24-30; 36-43: He put before them another parable: "The kingdom of heaven may be compared to someone who sowed good seed in his field; but while everybody was asleep, an enemy came and sowed weeds among the wheat, and then went away. So when the plants came up and bore grain, then the weeds appeared as well. And the slaves of the householder came and said to him, 'Master, did you not sow good seed in your field? Where, then, did these weeds come from?' He answered, 'An enemy has done this.' The slaves said to him, 'Then do you want us to go and gather them?' But he replied, 'No; for in gathering the weeds you would uproot the wheat along with them. Let both of them grow together until the harvest; and at harvest time I will tell the reapers, Collect the weeds first and bind them in bundles to be burned, but gather the wheat into my barn.'"

Then he left the crowds and went into the house. And his disciples approached him, saying, "Explain to us the parable of the weeds of the field." He answered, "The one who sows the good seed is the Son of Man; the field is the world, and the good seed are the children of the kingdom; the weeds are the children of the evil one, and the enemy who sowed them is the devil; the harvest is the end of the age, and the reapers are angels. Just as the weeds are collected and burned up with fire, so will it be at the end of the age. The Son of Man will send his angels, and they will collect out of his kingdom all causes of sin and all evildoers, and they will throw them into the furnace of fire, where there will be weeping and gnashing of teeth. Then the righteous will shine like the sun in the kingdom of their Father. Let anyone with ears listen!"

Do you ever wonder, as I do, why humanity's moral progress is so erratic? We have been seeking peace for hundreds of years, while at the same time we are developing more startling weapons of mass destruction. We find miraculous ways to send pictures through the air so they can be delivered in the loveliness of home or office, then we use this miracle to distribute inanities or moral filth. Our legislative bodies pass laws to eliminate economic corruption, but they can hardly keep ahead of those clever people who are finding ways to circumvent the laws as quickly as the laws are ratified.

Why can't our moral course be as straight-ahead as our mechanical progress? We don't have to reinvent the wheel in every generation. Science is still building on the seventeenth-century genius of Blaise Pascal. Gutenberg's moveable type has evolved to a world where typesetting is no longer necessary, and the modern counterparts to Marconi's primitive radio signals now carry pictures, color, and texture; why can't moral progress build, in the same fashion, from one generation to another? Maybe the prophet Micah was pondering the same sort of question twenty-seven centuries ago, when he asked,

> And what does the LORD require of you but to do justice, and to love kindness, and to walk humbly with your God? (Micah 6:8)

I think I catch a quality of exasperation in Micah's voice, as if he were saying, "Don't you get it? Do you have to be told the same thing time and again? Wasn't it enough that Moses gave the truth to you in the Law?"

Why don't we get it? Why doesn't one generation learn more from the previous ones? Why do we insist on burning our own fingers when we're warned that the stove is hot, and why aren't we willing to learn from our neighbor's experience without debacles of our own? Mark Twain had a point when he wrote, "Man is the only animal that blushes. Or needs to."

Perhaps Jesus' disciples were entertaining some variation of my question when Jesus told the parable of the weeds. As the Gospel of Matthew records it, Jesus had just explained the parable of the sower, the story of a farmer whose seed got a variety of receptions. Some of it fell on a roadway, where it was snatched up by birds; others on rocky ground, where it sprang up quickly but died just as quickly; while still more seed prospered until it was choked out by thorns. Only a small amount produced results, although the results were abundant.

I can imagine some disciples asking themselves about the thorns. Perhaps some of them asked specifically where the thorns came from, or perhaps Jesus anticipated the question that was in their minds. In any event, he told them another parable. The kingdom of heaven, he said, is like someone who has sown good seed in his field; "but while everybody was asleep, an enemy came and sowed weeds among the wheat and then went away" (Matthew 13:25). As the good seed and the weeds matured, the workers asked their master where the weeds had come from. I suspect they felt both bewildered and defensive. They had planted good seed; what had gone wrong? The master said simply, "An enemy has done this." The workers, practical folk, asked if they might pull up the weeds. Not yet, the master answered, because in rooting up the weeds some of the wheat might also be destroyed. "Let both of them grow together until the harvest"; then the showdown can come (Matthew 13:30).

A little later, when Jesus explained the parable to his disciples, he said that "the field is the world." Most of us will quickly answer, "No doubt about it." Our world is, indeed, a field of disparate fruits. The wheat and the weeds grow side by side. This is true in virtually every neighborhood, every school, and every business. There are people who are fruitful, and there are others who seem only to bring destruction. This doesn't surprise us; we're hardened to this fact, to the point that we take it for granted. But it's more unnerving when we see this mix of wheat and weeds within our own families. I remember a friend anticipating a family reunion; he not only wondered if some kin would come, he dreaded the prospect that some would do so. And while I'm pondering this anomaly, I have to acknowledge that it stretches even to the church. We like to refer to the church as the people of God; we say as much in our hymns and in our rituals. But in our candid moments we acknowledge that the old spiritual is right when it warns us that everyone who talks about heaven isn't going there. Not everyone who affiliates with the church, not even everyone who brings leadership to the church; not everyone, even, who is part of the church's ordained clergy is assuredly wheat. Weeds infiltrate the everyday reality of this body that, ideally, we describe as the body of Christ.

All of which compels us to recognize that this world of ours is caught in a massive conflict. There's a continuing battle between good and evil, and we're all part of it. It is the oldest conflict known to our human race, as old, biblically speaking, as the occasion when the serpent approached Adam and Eve in the Garden of Eden. I suspect this is the Bible's way of saying that this conflict has been with us always, and that it can manifest itself in even the most unlikely places—in our paradises, indeed. To be human is to be susceptible to this conflict; it is no respecter of age, of gender, of learning, of wealth, or of achievement. We never grow so learned as to be exempt from the battle, nor will old age allow us to retire from it.

This is, surely, as significant a part of our human story as anything any of us will know. Something in us humans wants terribly to be good; that's why we keep educating, passing laws, seeking remedies—we want things to be better than they are. But just as surely, something is out of order so that every step forward seems to be countered by a slipping backward. Our whole human story seems sometimes to be a Sisyphean tale; just when we think we've gotten the stone to the top of the slope, it frustrates us by rolling down again. There seems to be a contrariness in our universe. We sow good seed; and just when we feel most hopeful of the prospect of a crop of goodness, we discover weeds—some noxious creature that claims as much right to the soil as the seed we have so faithfully nurtured there.

Let me interrupt myself long enough to say that what is true of our civilization on a massive scale is equally true in our individual lives. Probably the apostle Paul is expressing something of this issue when he writes, "I do not understand my own actions. For I do not do what I want, but I do the very thing I hate" (Romans 7:15). Is there anyone who hasn't felt at times that he could have authored those words? We are encouraged to sow our lives with the good seed of Bible reading, church attendance, and consistent devotional practices, with the promise that these will eventuate in a life of spiritual beauty. But to our surprise and our huge discomfort, weeds appear. Whence these weeds, when we've worked so hard to produce loveliness? How is it that we can become irritated with common human actions just after we've received the Lord's Supper? The preacher has hardly finished a convincing point when a counterargument arises in the soul, such as, "You're not so perfect yourself." Sometimes the seed hardly has time to germinate before the weeds are choking it out.

So this much of the parable is clear: We are in a conflict! Our lives don't become fields of beauty and fruitfulness without a struggle. Some find this so discouraging that they simply quit trying. Unfortunately, some preaching doesn't prepare people for the struggle. People are led to believe that the way to heaven is one wonderful upward trail, not realizing that they will have to battle for nearly every inch gained. The Lord promised Joshua, "Every place that the sole of your foot will tread upon I have given to you," but then continued, "Be strong and courageous; do not be frightened or dismayed, for the LORD your God is with you wherever you go" (Joshua 1:3, 9). God had given the land to Joshua and his people, but they would have to conquer it if they were to get it. I suspect the same thing can be said for every conquest of the Christian life. I'm impressed that even the lovely Twenty-third Psalm acknowledges conflict: "You prepare a table before me / in the presence of my enemies" (Psalm 23:5).

Jesus leaves no doubt about the source of this problem. As he tells the story, when the farmer's servants ask where the weeds have come from, the owner answers, "An enemy has done this"; and if there is any confusion as to who this enemy is, Jesus settles the matter when he explains the parable to his disciples. He says quite directly, "The enemy who sowed [the weeds] is the devil" (Matthew 13:28, 39).

So what do we do about the weeds that appear in our human field? Just now I'm speaking not about the stuff that crops up in our personal lives, but in the community of faith. When we sow good seed in the world and expect to have a crop of praiseworthy believers, what do we do about the "weeds" in our midst? The Christian church has struggled with this question from its earliest days. We wish that all who claim to be Christians were wonderfully exemplary in life and conduct, but it is not so. Some religious bodies have specialized in standards that are rather easily measured; if membership is restricted to those who dress by a certain code or to those who fulfill certain clear patterns—tithing, for instance—then it is easy enough to determine the wheat from the weeds. But when the standard comes to matters of heart and intent, the distinctions are quite beyond most of us.

The householder's advice, therefore, was to leave the issue "to the end of the age," when the angel-reapers—qualified to make distinctions of such gravity—can separate the wheat from the weeds. Quite simply, only God is able to make the final judgments regarding good and evil. The great Saint Augustine said that in the Lord's field, "at times what was grain turns into weeds and at times what were weeds turn into grain; and no one knows what they will be tomorrow" (*Ancient Christian Commentary on Scripture; New Testament* Ia *Matthew 1–13* [Downers Grove, Ill.: InterVarsity

Press, 2001], page 277). My own long experience as a pastor confirms this judgment. Some persons I thought were weeds have proved in time to be God's fine wheat. Persons familiar with plant life in the Middle East tell us that there is a weed which, in its early stage, resembles wheat so closely that it is impossible to distinguish one from the other; and that when they have reached a point where the difference can be told, their roots are so intertwined that pulling up the weeds will tear out the wheat as well. What is true of the plant life seems surely to be true, in more dramatic ways, of saints and sinners in the church.

But how does this happen? How is it that God's good plans for our world and for our individual lives are so often thwarted? Granted that, as the householder in the parable said, "an enemy has done this"; and as Jesus explained, "the enemy...is the devil"; how does the enemy bring it about? How can we keep the devil from so often corrupting the world, our governments, our churches, and our individual lives?

Jesus said that it was "while everybody was asleep" that "an enemy came and sowed weeds among the wheat" (Matthew 13:25). So many of our problems develop, you know, while we're sleeping. Obviously I'm not referring to physical sleep. Physical sleep is essential to life, and we're soon in trouble if we don't get a proper share of it. I'm thinking rather of the kind of sleeping that afflicts our lives. This is the sort of thing the apostle Paul must have had in mind when he reminded the Christians in Thessalonica that they were "not of the night or of darkness," so it was expected that they would "keep awake and be sober" (1 Thessalonians 5:5-6).

So many of our world's problems happen while someone is sleeping. When I was a boy, Adolf Hitler was methodically and brutally destroying the Jewish people in Germany while America slept. Looking back on the period as history, one wonders how a civilized world could have allowed such monstrous events to happen. A woman whose husband had just said he wanted a divorce tried to tell me how their marriage had fallen apart. But she couldn't explain it. "I saw no signs," she said. "Everything seemed to be okay. I must have been asleep!" Specialists in the field of teenage drug prevention say that most cases could be prevented if only parents would catch the telltale signs in time. But the parents are often asleep; they're so occupied with making a living and planning for the future that they lose the very one who for them symbolizes the future.

And so it has been sometimes with my own soul. Few if any of the failures in my walk with God have come during days of hellish onslaught; they've happened while I've been sleeping. As the nineteenth-century Russian playwright Anton Chekhov put it, "Any idiot can face a crisis; it is this day-to-day living that wears you out." That's because we fall asleep in the day-to-day living while a crisis stabs us wide awake. Believe me, I prefer pleasant days over trouble, but I've slowly come to realize that I must be unusually alert during the pleasant days, else I will lose my soul to comfortable ordinariness.

The story Jesus told is so cataclysmic in its dimensions. The field, Jesus said, is the whole world; you can't get a much bigger stage. The one who sows the good seed is the Son of Man; you can't find a more passionately involved caretaker. The enemy is the devil; enough said as to the seriousness of the opposition. And the issue is of such a reach that it won't all be settled until "the end of the age." But it all hinges on this—what happens while everybody is asleep. How is it that something so eternally cataclysmic can tilt on so simple an issue?

It's enough to keep one awake at night. Or—to get to the heart of the matter—it's enough to keep us awake during the day.

CHAPTER 11

The Importance of Being Dressed for the Party

MATTHEW 22:1-14: Once more Jesus spoke to them in parables, saying: "The kingdom of heaven may be compared to a king who gave a wedding banquet for his son. He sent his slaves to call those who had been invited to the wedding banquet, but they would not come. Again he sent other slaves, saying, 'Tell those who have been invited: Look, I have prepared my dinner, my oxen and my fat calves have been slaughtered, and everything is ready; come to the wedding banquet.' But they made light of it and went away, one to his farm, another to his business, while the rest seized his slaves, maltreated them, and killed them. The king was enraged. He sent his troops, destroyed those murderers, and burned their city. Then he said to his slaves, 'The wedding is ready, but those invited were not worthy. Go therefore into the main streets, and invite everyone you find to the wedding banquet.' Those slaves went out into the streets and gathered all whom they found, both good and bad; so the wedding hall was filled with guests.

"But when the king came in to see the guests, he noticed a man there who was not wearing a wedding robe, and he said to him, 'Friend, how did you get in here without a wedding robe?' And he was speechless. Then the king said to the attendants, 'Bind him hand and foot, and throw him into the outer darkness, where there will be weeping and gnashing of teeth.' For many are called, but few are chosen."

If I had been one of Jesus' original disciples, I would have had some uncomfortable hours. Not during Jesus' teaching and preaching; that would have been all joy. And certainly not during his healing of the sick and his working of miracles; I would love to have been an observer at such times, cheering him on. It's all those parties. Jesus went to so many parties, and he told so many stories about parties, and I'm just not a good partygoer.

It's not that I don't love fun. I probably laugh more than any two or three people you know. I even laugh when I'm alone. I have to watch myself when I'm on airplanes, lest I chuckle too loudly while thinking, reading, or observing, and thus raise concern among my fellow passengers and flight attendants. It's just that I don't like organized frivolity and large groups. Put me in a conversation with no more than four people and I'm happy as a talkative clam, but take me to a party and unless someone intervenes I am soon alone in a corner, celebrating my solitude. Since this makes hostesses very nervous, it's better that I simply not go to parties. So I don't know how Jesus would have handled me. Perhaps there was another disciple like me; maybe Thaddaeus or Bartholomew (who was also known as Nathanael), since we don't hear much about them. I would have gravitated to them at all social occasions.

But I love the sense of overflowing joy that is inherent in Jesus' party parables. They tell me that our gospel is, indeed, good news, and that those who take it seriously are the happiest people you can find.

One of those party parables takes a peculiar turn, however. Just when Jesus brings us to the point where the combo is striking up the music and we're headed to the groaning table, he shows the host getting downright nasty. And worse, that's where the story ends.

Let me tell you about it. This parable seems aimed especially at the chief priests and Pharisees, who were becoming increasingly antagonistic to Jesus. The kingdom of heaven,

Jesus said, is like a king who was giving a wedding banquet for his son. We can see from the outset of this story that it's big business; after all, no social event could be much bigger than a wedding banquet for the king's son. With things nearly ready, the king sent out his servants to the previously invited guests, to tell them that the time had come. Strange to say, they ignored the king's invitation. The king then sent out another team, this time with a more insistent message: "Look, I have prepared my dinner, my oxen and my fat calves have been slaughtered, and everything is ready; come to the wedding banquet" (Matthew 22:4).

It's at this point in the story that we realize Jesus is describing a quite irrational situation. A good movie-maker could make the parable into a comedy of the absurd. This is a king who is being treated as if he were the host you try most to avoid. Following social protocol, he had sent an early invitation; and when the event was near, he sent his messengers to announce that the time had come. These messengers were ignored, so he sent still more, this time with an urgency that is somewhere between the ludicrous and the pathetic. Pathetic, if this were an ordinary host and hostess: the food almost ready and no one is here. "If they don't get here soon, the meat will get tough, the vegetables will lose their flavor, and the soufflé will collapse." But this is no ordinary household celebrating a son's wedding; this is the *king*! And the king is being made to look like a comic strip character. To make the situation still more absurd, Jesus notes that those who were invited "made light of it," some choosing to go to their farms, others to their businesses, and some—emboldened by the king's apparent helplessness—even mistreating and killing the slaves who had delivered the invitation.

Let me interrupt myself long enough to note that this portion of the parable no doubt has two applications. First, the parable describes the historic relationship between God and the people of Israel. Israel had been "invited" to God's abundance by the prophets—the slaves or servants in the parable—but Israel had been quite casual in their response. Sometimes, in fact, the response had been vicious, as in those instances when Israel killed the prophets—a matter referred to in Jesus' parable. The nation's failure reflected especially upon her religious leadership, the very ones that should have seen to it that the nation was ready for the "wedding feast."

But I'm sure the parable speaks to the church as well. For the past two millennia, God has looked to the church to do for the world what Israel was also called to do: to prepare the world for God's gracious rule. It has been our business to make ourselves and our culture ready for the kingdom of Christ. We haven't done very well. Like Israel, we've been pretty casual about God's invitation. It isn't enough that the secular culture has made martyrs; we've sometimes gotten into the martyring business ourselves, Catholics killing Reformers, and the Reformers, in turn, killing Catholics and sometimes other Reformers. But worse, even though not as dramatic, has been our continuing dullness of spirit. Only occasionally has the church been as vigorous, as loving, or as evangelistic as God must surely want it to be. So God's continuing banquet has been poorly attended; and the banquet to end all banquets, at the consummation of God's kingdom, seems indefinitely postponed.

Meanwhile, God has continued to recruit for the kingdom party. In the first instance, when Israel was slow to accept, God turned to the new body, the church. As one looks back on church history, one gets the impression that God is constantly forced to reach beyond those first invited to the party. That is, it seems to me that the church is constantly in need of renewal. We seem so quickly to become complacent, quite content to limit the party to our own kind. So a constant reforming and renewal has been going on, even to this present moment. Which is to say, God is going to have a party whether or not we have the sense to come and celebrate with him.

But then there's this last part of Jesus' story. It's the part I want particularly to discuss with you. When the party is in full swing, with joy and good feeling everywhere, the king notices a man there "who was not wearing a wedding robe" (Matthew 22:11). The mood changes dramatically. The king asks, "Friend, how did you get in here without a wedding robe?" (Matthew 22:12). The man is speechless. The king orders that the man be bound "hand and foot," and thrown into "outer darkness, where there will be weeping and gnashing of teeth" (Matthew 22:13).

Earlier in this story the king was so anxious for a party that he not only enlarged his guest list, he all but compelled persons to come. How is it that the expansive host has now become a vindictive enforcer of a dress code? The servants who once were on the streets begging people to come to the party are now called to throw out a guest. The difference in the king's attitude is shocking. In truth, when I watched him sending out his team to recruit guests, I thought he wasn't interested in qualifications, and that he wanted only to fill the seats at the banquet table. What is the meaning in this bizarre turn of events?

Saints and scholars of other times have wrestled with the question. The great Saint Augustine said that the wedding garment was a matter of the heart not of the body, else the servants would have noticed the irregularity. He felt therefore that it was the garment of righteousness. Gregory the Great warned, in one of his sermons, that since we have come into the house of the marriage feast by way of God's generosity, we should be careful lest some fault be found in our heart's clothing. For him, the measure of the garment was love.

I need not tell you that I'm not as wise as Augustine or Gregory the Great, but I have read a lot of theology by observing human nature, both in myself and in my fellow pilgrims. I won't insist that what I'm about to say is the essential point of the parable, but it is a point that may do us good.

The parable makes clear that the guests who finally came

to the party got there by grace. The king instructed his servants to go into the main streets and to "invite everyone you find," and we read that those who were gathered together for the grand occasion were "both good and bad" (Matthew 22:9-10). This was not a select group. It is a group that reminds one of gracious words from the last chapter in our Bible: "Let anyone who wishes take the water of life as a gift" (Revelation 22:17). The king's net had been thrown out and drawn in indiscriminately. People didn't qualify for the invitation; the invitation qualified them.

But grace, that indescribable gift, has a hidden peril. By definition, *grace* is undeserved favor. But we humans find it difficult to see any favor as undeserved. Something in us insists on believing there must be *some* merit in us that has brought about the favor we've received. And while most of us would at least be careful not to verbalize such a feeling, we might easily make a tacit expression of that feeling by becoming presumptuous. A bit of folk wisdom that is at least as old as the fifth century in the Latin reminds us that "familiarity breeds contempt." In the world of faith, familiarity generally stops short of contempt; it stops at the home of contempt's near neighbor, presumption.

I think of the fearful Old Testament story of Nadab and Abihu, sons of the first high priest, Aaron. Not only was Aaron their father, Moses was their uncle. They saw God's miracles close-up, at the Red Sea and at Mount Sinai. They were among the select group of seventy persons who had a kind of private audience with the Lord God. But it seems they grew so comfortable with holy things that one day they appeared at the altar intoxicated, and suffered the dramatic judgment of God. They enjoyed so much of God's favor that they took it for granted. They grew presumptuous. (See Leviticus 10:1-3, 8-11.)

In dictionary definitions of *presume* or *presumption,* "to take for granted" is one of the first phrases you'll see. Presumption is a hazard in every relationship, human or divine. We long for a level of friendship that means someone will accept us as we are, faults and all; but if we get such a friendship, it's very easy to presume upon it. Even the best and most patient friend doesn't want to be taken for granted. Presumption is one of the greatest perils of marriage, though it is rarely mentioned. A man and a woman commit their lives to one another because they feel that no other person in the world could mean so much to them. But living together day and night, year after year, through varieties of experiences and of mutual humanness can make even the most remarkable man and the most winsome woman seem ordinary; and with that seeming, presumption can enter in. When Madame Anne Bigot de Cornuel (1605–1694) said, "No man is a hero to his valet," I suspect she was indicating that all of us have flaws that will be revealed if only someone spends enough time with us. God has no flaws, but even God can be taken for granted. And this is especially so when God shows us the unmerited favor of grace. We are all too likely to think we have some peculiar appeal to the divine, else why would God be so good to us?

So I wonder if this guest in Matthew 22:11-14 took his invitation for granted. Since the invitation had been so insistent, did he reason that he must be very special? In that case, why worry about wardrobe? Surely the king would want him no matter what he wore.

Whatever else this parable is teaching, I'm sure this is an element: It was unthinkable arrogance to come to a king's banquet improperly dressed. This is probably a little difficult for our currently casual culture to understand, but through most of history there have been dress codes—even among the most common and impoverished. Indeed, sometimes the poor have been more concerned about such codes than those who were more comfortably situated. The guest in our parable somehow thought he could get by, that the rules didn't apply to him.

It's a danger to which we are all susceptible. Professional religious workers like myself can easily lose the sense of God's otherness; the altar, the bread and wine, the Book, the rituals—all these can become so commonplace that without our knowing it we take *mysterium tremendum*—the tremendous mystery—for granted and become presumptuous. The longtime church member, of whom we say, "She's held every office in the church," can come to feel that the church is her property—and by unconscious extension, that God is her property, too. Under such circumstances, it's easy to think that what we want for the church is what's right, period. Presumption comes subtly but all too easily. The wonder of grace can slip into an attitude of entitlement.

In the seminary where I teach, Charles Wesley's hymn "And Can It Be that I Should Gain" is our declaration for all special occasions. The concluding verse includes the powerful line, "Bold I approach / th'eternal throne." One of the godliest persons I know remains silent on that line. "I have no right to be bold," he explained to me. "I dare not make such a claim." I might be able to argue the point with him theologically, but his spirit is right; God save us from presumption.

I am struck by the way the king in the parable addresses the guilty party. "Friend," the king says. "*Friend.*" I don't mean to build a doctrinal case on a single word, but at least there's an insight to be considered. This person who came in an improper garment was not a stranger. As Jesus tells the story, the king addressed him with the same word Jesus used when Judas betrayed him: "Friend" (Matthew 26:50). This guest knew better than to dress as he did. The garments of presumption have no place in the dominions of grace.

God's love is, as the poet said, broader than the measure of man's mind. But God is God, and we are not; and we should never forget that ultimate distinction. And especially, we should never presume upon grace.

CHAPTER 12

The Genius of Effective Waiting

LUKE 12:32-40: "Do not be afraid, little flock, for it is your Father's good pleasure to give you the kingdom. Sell your possessions, and give alms. Make purses for yourselves that do not wear out, an unfailing treasure in heaven, where no thief comes near and no moth destroys. For where your treasure is, there your heart will be also.

"Be dressed for action and have your lamps lit; be like those who are waiting for their master to return from the wedding banquet, so that they may open the door for him as soon as he comes and knocks. Blessed are those slaves whom the master finds alert when he comes; truly I tell you, he will fasten his belt and have them sit down to eat, and he will come and serve them. If he comes during the middle of the night, or near dawn, and finds them so, blessed are those slaves.

"But know this: if the owner of the house had known at what hour the thief was coming, he would not have let his house be broken into. You also must be ready, for the Son of Man is coming at an unexpected hour."

Waiting is hard work. Ask any child who is counting the days until Christmas, or any couple marking time until their wedding. Or ask someone who is anticipating an especially cherished vacation, or a commencement day for themselves or someone in the family. We are futurists, all of us, and it's hard work.

Waiting is at its most difficult when that for which we are waiting has no definite deadline. That's why futuring is such a big business. Fascination with the future is no doubt as old as the human race, and the practice of futuring ranges from the primitive to the scholarly, with some areas along the way where it's hard to tell one from the other. Hundreds of generations have looked to the stars to estimate the future, and I suppose there have been variations on the reading of tea leaves in scores of cultures over centuries of time. Contemporary business, government, industry, and scholarship explore the future with careful, documented studies that then leap off into the space of speculation. Thousands of new products appear on our grocery shelves each year on the basis of someone's futuring, and most of the thousands prove to be futile speculation. No baseball season could begin without specialists giving odds as to who will end up in the World Series, and the college football and basketball seasons enter each week with a revised list of the top twenty-five teams. All of it has to do with our fascination with the future.

But these matters are child's play compared to our fascination with the ultimate future of our human race. Whether we use the term "the second coming of Christ," or the more general, secular term "the end of the world," no subject has a more enduring appeal. A person may be praying for the consummation or dreading it, but the appeal is the same. And whether dread or desire, the waiting is hard work.

When you read the Old Testament, you find that "How long" is one of the most popular phrases with the prophets and the writers of the psalms. In some instances they were awaiting God's intervention at a personal level and at others on a cosmic scale, but especially the writers pleaded to know how much longer they would have to wait before God would set things right. The New Testament takes up the same theme, but with a sharper focus. Jesus spoke freely about "the end of the age." And although he gave broad hints about when this consummation might be, he seemed always to conclude such remarks by saying something like, "the Son of Man is coming at an unexpected hour" (Matthew 24:44). That uncertainty makes waiting all the more difficult.

No wonder, then, that the theme never seems to lose its appeal. When the disciples asked Jesus, "Tell us, when will this be?" (Matthew 24:3), they were picking up where the prophets and psalmists had left off; and we have continued to raise the question for nearly two thousand years since then. You can see how compelling a question it is these days, when you consider how a series of fiction books dealing with the subject has sold millions of copies, setting sales marks that would be phenomenal for books in any field. But this is nothing new. Nearly thirty-five years ago, a book that attempted to predict the time of Christ's return, *The Late Great Planet Earth,* was published; it has sold more than eighteen million copies. In my boyhood, *In the Twinkling of an Eye,* a fiction book on the same topic enjoyed huge popularity for many years. And if you want to go back further still, people became so excited in the year 999, when they reasoned that probably Christ would come or the world would end in the year 1000, that pilgrims filled the roads to Jerusalem so they would be present to greet their Lord at his coming.

Obviously, the subject of eschatology (to use the theological term), or "the end of the world" (to use a popular but incorrect term), has been badly mistreated over the centuries, up to and including the present time. It has become the happy hunting ground for a good deal of irresponsible preaching and teaching, both religious and secular. But that's no reason to avoid the subject. Rather, it should remind us that this is an important subject, in fact, a terribly and wonderfully important one. People preach about it and write books about it because it matters so much to all of us. Jesus said a very great deal about this subject, so if we profess to care about what Jesus said, we have reason to think about it, too.

It's in that mood that we look at one of the instances when Jesus approached the subject through a parable. He had been telling his disciples not to worry. "For life is more than food," Jesus said, "and the body more than clothing" (Luke 12:23). He pleaded with them not to strive after the things that occupy the time and minds and affections of the world around us. Then he spoke a word of wonderful reassurance: "Do not be afraid, little flock," he said, "for it is your Father's good pleasure to give you the kingdom" (Luke 12:32). The kingdom was just what they were waiting for—the future God had planned—so they were ready for the story Jesus told them.

He described a group of servants who were waiting for their master to return from a wedding banquet. They were so anxious for his return that they were poised to open the door as soon as he might knock. Such persons, Jesus said, are blessed, because when the master finds such alertness, "he will fasten his belt and have them sit down to eat, and he will come and serve them" (Luke 12:37). It is a quite extraordinary picture. In the first-century Middle East it was the servants who tucked their garments under the belt to make it easier for them to scurry about their serving, but Jesus portrays a master so pleased about the attitude of his servants that he reverses the normal order. He tells his servants to recline to eat, while he fastens his belt so he can serve them!

But there is good reason for the master's sense of pleasure. These are servants, Jesus says, who are so dedicated that their master can come "during the middle of the night, or near dawn," and he will find them alert and waiting. They don't have any off times. There's no hour when they stop expecting. At this point in his story, however, Jesus changes both the mood and the figure of speech. If the owner of a house had known when a thief was coming, Jesus said, he wouldn't have allowed his house to be broken into.

So, he continued, "You also must be ready, for the Son of Man is coming at an unexpected hour" (Luke 12:39-40).

Now there's the rub! Our Lord's return is going to be "at an unexpected hour." That's what makes waiting so difficult, so frustrating, and so tiring. We have no idea when this consummation is going to be. Suppose you're setting up a strategic appointment—a wedding, or a meeting with a loan officer, or a visit from the recruiting coach for the team your son or daughter wants to play for:

"When can I expect you?"

"When you don't expect me."

"I mean—could we set a time?"

"Sure. Put me down for 'an unexpected hour.'"

That's really quite maddening, isn't it!

So of course we keep trying to calculate when that "unexpected hour" will be. Preachers and earnest Bible students search the Scriptures to see if they can locate some obscure text, some exotic symbol, or perhaps some exciting juxtaposition of numbers that will reveal the time. But Jesus said no one could know. "But about that day and hour no one knows, neither the angels of heaven, nor the Son, but only the Father" (Matthew 24:36). Isn't it interesting that people who profess Christ as Lord keep seeking information that Jesus said was simply unavailable?

Mind you, Jesus gave a hint. Just after he said that no one but God knows the day or the hour, he continued, "For as the days of Noah were, so will be the coming of the Son of Man. For as in those days before the flood they were eating and drinking, marrying and giving in marriage, until the day Noah entered the ark, and they knew nothing until the flood came and swept them all away, so too will be the coming of the Son of Man" (Matthew 24:37-39). So what was Jesus telling his disciples? Simply this, that people were unprepared for the flood because life was going along in such a normal way. There could be no better picture of predictable life than this, "eating and drinking, marrying and giving in marriage." That's the way life is; we eat and drink, we marry and continue into another generation. No wonder Noah's contemporaries were unprepared for disaster when life was so normal! And so it will be, Jesus said, before his return. Things will be normal: People will be eating and drinking, marrying and moving on into the next generation. No wonder, then, that Jesus said on that occasion, as on several others, "Therefore you also must be ready, for the Son of Man is coming at an unexpected hour" (Matthew 24:44). There it is again—that word, *unexpected!*

Why didn't Jesus give us more hard data? It hardly seems fair that he would expect us to be ready for his coming when we have no idea when it will be. On several occasions Jesus compared himself to a bridegroom coming to meet his bride. What kind of person would expect the bride to be ready at any time? The answer: the Eternal Bridegroom. We want to say, "Can't you at least give us a *hint* about when you're coming?" And the answer is, "No; that's the very point. I'm looking for a bride who is so committed to me that she will be ready whenever I appear."

The point is really quite obvious. God is expecting *faithfulness* in us. To return to the figure of speech in our parable, any servant, including the most inferior, will be good when he expects his work to be inspected or when he knows the master is going to appear. But the *quality* servant is ready at all times. Whether the master is coming or is delayed, this quality servant works and lives with the same level of dedication and faithfulness. That's the point of the matter.

And that, believe me, is hard work. Waiting is hard work, when you have no idea when the point of your waiting will be fulfilled.

Well, we've been waiting now for nearly two thousand years. It's clear that when the apostle Paul wrote to the church at Thessalonica midway in the first century, he thought Christ might return at any time. It appears that some Thessalonians were so sure of this that they may have quit their jobs, simply to wait. And we're still waiting. Some earnest believers are waiting for the "archangel's call and . . . the sound of God's trumpet" (1 Thessalonians 4:16). Others are waiting for a kingdom that will come to pass like the working of leaven in the dough of our world (Matthew 13:33). One way or another, a great many of us are waiting. And a great many of us testify to our waiting, probably without fully realizing what we're saying, when we announce in the ritual of Holy Communion, "Christ has died; Christ is risen; Christ will come again."

When? When is our Lord coming? Are we Christian believers little more than those tragicomic characters Vladimir and Estragon in Samuel Beckett's play, who spend their lives waiting for Godot? In the play, Godot keeps sending word that he will appear, but he never does. Are we Christians waiting in just such futile fashion?

By no means! But I do have a feeling that much of our waiting has been in an inadequate fashion. I return to the setting in which Jesus spoke the parable. Jesus said, "Do not be afraid, little flock, for it is your Father's good pleasure to give you the kingdom. Sell your possessions, and give alms. Make purses for yourselves that do not wear out, an unfailing treasure in heaven. . . . For where your treasure is, there your heart will be also" (Luke 12:32-34). And it was from this base that Jesus told his disciples—including us—to be "dressed for action," so we would be ready for our master to return (Luke 12:35-36).

In other words, if we believe in the kingdom of God, we will live with Kingdom values. We will live as if this world is not the end of it all. Instead of accumulating still more—which is very much the standard of this world—we will "sell [our] possessions," so we can give more away. We will buy Kingdom-style purses, the kind that will hold heaven's unfailing treasures; goodness knows that our current purses—our mutual funds and properties and antiques—won't make it to the other side, so we had better get purses that will! Quite simply, we will begin putting more and more of our treasures in heaven; and before we know it, our hearts will follow our treasures, because—as Jesus said—where your treasure is, that's soon where your heart will be.

Here, in a sense, is the very essence of prophecy: Have your treasures in the right place. This is the ultimate point about everything concerning the second coming of Christ, that we should have our treasures where they belong, in the acts of kindness, charity, evangelism, and loving sacrifice that characterize God's kingdom.

Then when will the Lord come? I don't know! But I do know that I want to be living in the style of God's kingdom. And that means that I will be ready for the party, whenever it comes.

You see, there are some things we don't know, and that Jesus said we never will know. We don't know when he will return. We only know that it will be like a thief in the night. You don't know when a thief is coming; that's the nature of the thief's business—and Jesus said that his return will be in that style. So, no, I don't know when he is coming.

But I do know how to be ready. The secret is to be so in love with God and God's purposes that we don't get unduly attached to this world. Therefore, whenever he comes, we'll be ready. And here's still another thing we know: that God is so pleased with those who are faithful that when the Master comes, he will tuck his robe in his belt so that he can wait tables for us! Because, Jesus said, it is God's *pleasure* to give us the Kingdom!

Do we need to know anything more than that? No. So let's get ready. We don't know when it will be, but we'll be dressed for the party, whenever. And in the meanwhile, we'll be living in Kingdom style.

SUGGESTIONS FOR LEADING A STUDY OF

More Parables from the Back Side

JOHN D. SCHROEDER

This book by J. Ellsworth Kalas takes familiar parables—stories Jesus told to teach lessons—and looks at them from another side, from a different angle. To assist you in facilitating a discussion group, this study guide was created to help make this experience beneficial both for you and for the members of your group. Here are some thoughts on how you can help your group:

1. Distribute the book to participants before your first meeting and request that they come having read the first chapter. You may want to limit the size of your group to increase participation.
2. Begin your sessions on time. Your participants will appreciate your promptness. You may wish to begin your first session with introductions and a brief get-acquainted time. Start each session by reading aloud the snapshot summary of the chapter for the day.
3. Select discussion questions and activities in

advance. Note that the first question usually is a general question designed to get discussion going. The last question often is designed to summarize the discussion. Feel free to change the order of the listed questions and to create your own questions. Allow a set amount of time for the questions and activities.

4. Remind your participants that all questions are valid as part of the learning process. Encourage their participation in discussion by saying that there are no "wrong" answers and that all input will be appreciated. Invite participants to share their thoughts, personal stories, and ideas as their comfort level allows.
5. Some questions may be more difficult to answer than others. If you ask a question and no one responds, begin the discussion by venturing an answer yourself. Then ask for comments and other answers. Remember that some questions may have multiple answers.
6. Ask the question "Why?" or "Why do you believe that?" to help continue a discussion and give it greater depth.
7. Give everyone a chance to talk. Keep the conversation moving. Occasionally you may want to direct a question to a specific person who has been quiet. "Do you have anything to add?" is a good follow-up question to ask another person. If the topic of conversation gets off track, move ahead by asking the next question in your study guide.
8. Before moving from questions to activities, ask group members if they have any questions that have not been answered. Remember that as a leader, you do not have to know all the answers. Some answers may come from group members. Other answers may even need a bit of research. Your

job is to keep the discussion moving and to encourage participation.

9. Review the activity in advance. Feel free to modify it or to create your own activity. Encourage participants to try the "At home" activity.
10. Following the conclusion of the activity, close with a brief prayer, praying either the printed prayer from the study guide or a prayer of your own. If your group desires, pause for individual prayer petitions.
11. Be grateful and supportive. Thank group members for their ideas and participation.
12. You are not expected to be a "perfect" leader. Just do the best you can by focusing on the participants and the lesson. God will help you lead this group.
13. Enjoy your time together!

SUGGESTIONS FOR PARTICIPANTS

1. What you will receive from this study will be in direct proportion to your involvement. Be an active participant!
2. Please make it a point to attend all sessions and to arrive on time so that you can receive the greatest benefit.
3. Read the chapter and review the study guide questions prior to the meeting. You may want to jot down questions you have from the reading, and also answers to some of the study guide questions.
4. Be supportive and appreciative of your group leader as well as the other members of your group. You are on a journey together.
5. Your participation is encouraged. Feel free to share your thoughts about the material being discussed.
6. Pray for your group and your leader.

1. The Value of the House

SNAPSHOT SUMMARY

This chapter looks at the choices we make in life, and the need for building our lives upon a strong foundation.

REFLECTION / DISCUSSION QUESTIONS

1. Share why you have selected this book to read or what you hope to learn from it.
2. What lessons about life can be learned from studying this parable?
3. Share a time when you made a decision that turned out not to be wise.
4. List some of the storms of life that are common to many or most people. Give an example of a storm you experienced.
5. Explain why Jesus used the harsh word *foolish* in this parable.
6. Give some reasons why people build lives upon "sand" instead of a better foundation.
7. How is the human body like a house?
8. Name some of the characteristics of a life built upon a strong foundation.
9. What does this parable tell you about Jesus and his values?
10. Name a wise way and a foolish way of accomplishing a specific task.

ACTIVITIES

As a group: How many choices does a person make each day? To gain a glimpse of this answer, give each person paper and a pencil and ask them to write down the names of choices they make between 6 A.M. and noon (or between noon and 6 P.M.) on a normal weekday.

Compare lists. Who made the most choices? What governs how these choices were made?

At home: Reflect on the choices you make concerning your body, your mind, and your spirit. Consider changing foolish behavior, and outline a plan to do so.

Prayer: *Dear God, thank you for giving us the freedom of choice. Help us to make wise choices and to build our lives upon a firm foundation. Remind us that you are with us during the storms of life, and that your love goes with us each day. Amen.*

2. The Man Who Talked with His Soul

SNAPSHOT SUMMARY

This chapter shows why it is crucial that our spirituality is centered on God and includes a focus on others, rather than being focused on us alone.

REFLECTION / DISCUSSION QUESTIONS

1. Name the ways in which the man in the parable was remarkable, smart, and successful.
2. What did the man in the parable leave out of his life? What clues are there that he was concerned only about himself?
3. What does it mean that the man "talked with his soul"? How might we phrase that today?
4. What lessons about spiritual needs can be learned from this parable?
5. Why do you think the villains in many of Jesus' parables were spiritual people? What does this tell us?

6. In what ways are many Christians today similar to the man in the parable?
7. In your own words, explain what greed means, and how a person guards against it. Is greed ever good? Explain your answer.
8. What do you think the author meant by his statement, "It is very difficult to be rich and still keep your balance"? What do you think possibly could cause a person who is wealthy to lose ties with reality?
9. Aside from financial wealth, what makes people rich?
10. What key learning from this chapter will you most reflect on in your personal life today/this week?

ACTIVITIES

As a group: Give participants Bibles, and ask them to locate different examples where Jesus was critical of a spiritual person. Compile a list of what the spiritual people were doing wrong.

At home: Reflect on how you are like the rich man in the parable. Are you making the same mistakes? What commitment will you make to change?

Prayer: *Dear God, thank you for the many gifts and blessings you provide. Help us not to be so caught up in our belongings that we forget you and others. Remind us of the importance of people around us, and show us how to pass along your love and blessings. Amen.*

3. What Chance Does an Average Sinner Have?

SNAPSHOT SUMMARY

This chapter illustrates how the grace of God is freely offered to *all* sinners.

REFLECTION / DISCUSSION QUESTIONS

1. What lessons did you learn from this parable?
2. How did Simon neglect Jesus, and why do you think he did so? How did the woman in the parable make up for Simon's neglect?
3. How did the woman act both inappropriately and appropriately?
4. In what ways is Simon's situation like our own situation in life?
5. Why did Jesus "apply" or spell out his parable for Simon?
6. Where do you see yourself in this parable, and why?
7. How did sinful Simon and the sinful woman perceive Jesus differently, and why?
8. What did you learn about the grace of God from reading this lesson?
9. Who are the "tax collectors" and sinners of our day with whom Jesus would associate?
10. What chance does God give the "average sinner"? In your own words, summarize this lesson.

ACTIVITIES

As a group: Use your church library or other resources to explore the lives of Charles Wesley, John Newton, and Teresa of Avila. Ask each group member to discover and share a fact about one of these individuals.

At home: Share something you learned from this lesson with someone this week.

Prayer: *Dear God, thank you for the opportunity to learn more about your amazing grace that is offered to us all. We all need your forgiveness; help us not to be blind to our own needs. Guide our thoughts, words, and deeds so that they may be pleasing to you. Amen.*

4. The Importance of Downward Mobility

SNAPSHOT SUMMARY

This chapter takes a look at the topics of humility and social practices.

REFLECTION / DISCUSSION QUESTIONS

1. Give a definition and example of *humility*. Why is humility a good quality?
2. Share a time when you were humbled.
3. Name some of the lessons that can be learned from this parable.
4. Explain why there is no real fulfillment through self-promotion.
5. List some of the reasons people may lack humility.
6. Why do godliness and goodness matter more than other achievements?
7. Reflect on or discuss what you believe Jesus' ideal dinner-party guest list would look like. Who would be included?
8. What does this parable tell us about God?
9. What messages is Jesus trying to tell us in this parable about our social practices?

10. What practical applications does this parable have for business life or work life, and for church life?

ACTIVITIES

As a group: As a group, plan and implement the serving of a meal for persons who are homeless (or a similar activity that promotes humbleness).

At home: Practice being a servant this week. Aim for being last instead of first.

Prayer: *Dear God, thank you for reminding us of the importance of humility. Help us to put others ahead of ourselves. Lower our ego and increase our desire to promote and encourage others. Show us the true meaning of being your disciple. Amen.*

5. The Danger of Being Good and Empty

SNAPSHOT SUMMARY

This chapter shows that it's not enough just to be "clean" and "good"; we need God to make us *full.*

REFLECTION / DISCUSSION QUESTIONS

1. Share a lesson you learned from reading this chapter.
2. Explain your concept of a good person.
3. Share your idea of what it means to be a "good and empty" person.
4. What is dangerous about being good and empty?
5. What does "a good life" mean to you? Give an example.

6. Share a time when you felt empty. Explain what emptiness feels like.
7. What makes a person empty? What does an empty person lack?
8. What was meant by the words "unclean spirit"?
9. Where does fullness come from? Explain why.
10. Why did Jesus tell this story? What was the main point he wanted to convey?

ACTIVITIES

As a group: Give pencils and paper to group members. Ask each person to write down ten characteristics of a full person and ten characteristics of an empty person. Compare lists, with an emphasis on tips for how to be a full person.

At home: Reflect on your goodness. Are you good and empty or good and full? What makes you this way? What changes may be needed in your life? What commitments will you make to bring about those changes?

Prayer: *Dear God, thank you for filling us with your love. Help us remember that fullness comes from a close relationship with Jesus Christ and an active faith. Increase our capacity to be good to others and to share your love. Amen.*

6. Risky Business

SNAPSHOT SUMMARY

This chapter examines the cost of following Jesus and shows why it is worth the risks.

REFLECTION / DISCUSSION QUESTIONS

1. Explain the meaning of the parable. Who is the merchant? Who or what is the pearl?
2. How can you apply this parable to daily life?
3. What did you learn about Jesus from this parable?
4. Share a time when you took a risk. Explain why the risk was taken.
5. List some of the costs and risks of following Jesus and making a commitment.
6. Explain what you think of or how you feel when you see or hear the word *repent*. What image comes to mind?
7. What is the price to gain the kingdom of heaven?
8. Why don't many Christians talk about the risks or the price of the Kingdom? What statements are made instead?
9. How did God take a risk on us, and why did God do so?
10. Explain what it means that proof only goes so far, and after that you go on faith. Give an example of this.

ACTIVITIES

As a group: Give paper and a marker or crayon to each group member. Ask each person to create a bumper sticker design of eight words or less that reflects this lesson.

At home: Reflect on the risks you take in your life. Consider what risks you are willing to take on behalf of your faith.

Prayer: *Dear God, thank you for the wisdom behind this parable. Help us to remember that you risked your only son, Jesus, for us in order that we may have eternal life. Grant us courage to take risks on behalf of our faith. Amen.*

7. Miracles Can Be Overrated

SNAPSHOT SUMMARY

This chapter teaches that the Scriptures are more important than miracles in leading us to godly living.

REFLECTION / DISCUSSION QUESTIONS

1. How do you feel after reading this parable, and why?
2. What expectations does God have for people who have wealth?
3. Explain what is suggested by the lack of a name for the rich man.
4. Share a time when you felt like a "have-not." How does it feel to lack something you need?
5. What can you learn about God from this parable?
6. How would you define a miracle? Have you ever experienced one? If so, briefly describe it.
7. List and reflect on/discuss some reasons people seek miracles.
8. Explain the connection between faith and miracles.
9. Why is scripture better than miracles, according to Jesus?
10. Name some lessons about life and faith that come from this parable.

ACTIVITIES

As a group: Make a list of some simple ways you can help persons who are in need. Ask each member of the group to select a method and to commit to helping a person in need this week. Ask participants to be prepared to give a brief report on their efforts during the next group meeting.

At home: Think about how much you have been given, and how you can share some of your riches with others.

Prayer: *Dear God, thank you for all you have given us. Thank you for food, clothing, health, employment, shelter, family. Help us to share the blessings we have, and open our eyes to the needs of others. Thank you for all that you have given us to guide us in our faith without the need to see a miracle every day. Amen.*

8. Second Chance for a Poor Manager

SNAPSHOT SUMMARY

This chapter shows how God wants us to use creativity, imagination, and determination in our service to him.

REFLECTION / DISCUSSION QUESTIONS

1. What insights or lessons did you learn from this parable?
2. Reflect on/discuss the ways in which many people today are like the manager in the parable. What are the commonalities?
3. The author notes that this parable is strange compared to many other parables. Reflect on/discuss how this parable is different.
4. What aspects of this parable have multiple interpretations? Explain them.
5. Share a time when you were given a second chance or had the opportunity to offer a second chance to someone. How did it feel? What were the results?
6. List ways in which the manager showed creativity and wisdom.
7. Why were the Pharisees offended by this parable?
8. How does this parable challenge you?

9. What do we learn about God from this parable?
10. What qualities does God seek in workers to build God's kingdom?

ACTIVITIES

As a group: Identify a problem or a need at church or within your community, then as a group use creativity and imagination to tackle it. (If necessary, begin this activity this week and set aside a few minutes next week to continue planning or provide a progress report.)

At home: Take an inventory of your talents. Reflect on how you can use them more creatively in the service of God.

Prayer: *Dear God, thank you for the imagination and creativity that we all have inside of us. Help us to use these abilities to further your kingdom. Remind us to think of others, rather than ourselves. May we share your love and compassion with those who are in need. Amen.*

9. A Laugh and a Prayer

SNAPSHOT SUMMARY

This chapter teaches us to persist in prayer, even when circumstances are negative.

REFLECTION / DISCUSSION QUESTIONS

1. What practical applications for life are contained in these parables?
2. Give some reasons it is important to be persistent.

3. Share a time when you were persistent. What helped you remain focused?
4. When is laughter appropriate in prayer?
5. What is necessary in order for God's will to occur?
6. Give some examples of things that happen that are not of God's will.
7. Reflect on / discuss how humor can help in times of difficulty.
8. Share a time when a prayer of yours was answered.
9. Why does God sometimes say "no" to a prayer request? List some possible reasons.
10. How does it feel when a prayer is not answered? What can you do? How should you respond?

ACTIVITIES

As a group: Give pencils and paper to group members and ask them to write a prayer of five sentences or less that contains the words *laughter* and *persistence.* Share your prayers.

At home: Examine your prayer life: Are you practicing persistence? Is there a place in your praying for humor?

Prayer: *Dear God, thank you for the power of laughter and prayer. Together, they lighten our load and lift our spirits. Help us to continue to come to you in prayer and to persist in asking for your intervention in our lives and our world. May we not be discouraged, but boldly ask for your blessings. Grant us wisdom to ask for what we need. We know you will respond in love. Amen.*

10. It Happens While We Sleep

SNAPSHOT SUMMARY

This chapter examines the battle between good and evil in our world, and the risk of being spiritually asleep.

REFLECTION / DISCUSSION QUESTIONS

1. Give your own definitions of *good* and *evil.*
2. List some of the practical applications to life and faith found in this parable.
3. What can you learn about God from this parable?
4. What often prevents people from distinguishing between "weeds" and "wheat"?
5. Where do you think the mix of weeds and wheat is most apparent in the world or in a profession?
6. How should you cope with the "weeds" that come into your life?
7. Share a time when something bad happened when you were "sleeping" or not paying attention.
8. What evidence do you see that evil is real and at work in this world?
9. Life is a struggle. Share a struggle you have faced. How has God helped you fight the battles of life?
10. List and reflect on/discuss ways in which you can sow good seeds at home, at work, and at church.

ACTIVITIES

As a group: Use newspapers or magazines to locate stories about "weeds" mixed in with the "wheat." Share your findings.

At home: Reflect on the weeds and the wheat in your life and within your community. Think about how you can encourage good works in others.

Prayer: *Dear God, thank you for this parable and for the insights gained from it. Help us to eliminate the negatives in our lives and in our world, and to replace them with positives. Open our eyes to the weeds around us. Show us how to love others as you love us. Amen.*

11. The Importance of Being Dressed for the Party

SNAPSHOT SUMMARY

This chapter offers a reminder not to take God or God's grace for granted.

REFLECTION / DISCUSSION QUESTIONS

1. In your own words, explain the meaning of this parable.
2. What does this parable tell us about the God and God's grace?
3. List some practical applications for your spiritual life from this parable.
4. How does this parable describe the relationship between God and Israel?
5. In what way does this parable describe the church?
6. What did the author mean by his statement, "We [the church] seem so quickly to become complacent, quite content to limit the party to our own kind"?
7. Why did the king reject an invited guest? What message did Jesus want us to get from this?
8. List reasons why people reject God's invitation.
9. In what ways are we like the invited guests in the parable?
10. Reflect on/discuss the dangers of presumption as it applies to this parable and to our lives.

ACTIVITIES

As a group: Use Bibles or hymnals to locate and list ten or more aspects or traits of God's grace.
At home: Read this parable again, and reflect upon its meaning for your life.

Prayer: *Dear God, thank you for your grace. You love us, accept us, forgive us, and bless us, although we do not deserve it. Help us to respond to your grace with love for you and for others. Guide our actions so that they may be pleasing to you and be a blessing to those in need. Amen.*

12. The Genius of Effective Waiting

SNAPSHOT SUMMARY

This chapter provides insights into waiting for and preparing for God's kingdom.

REFLECTION / DISCUSSION QUESTIONS

1. List some practical applications of this parable to daily life.
2. What factors often make it difficult to wait for something or someone?
3. Share a time when you had difficulty waiting.
4. Why is eschatology, the study of the end times, an important subject? How is it sometimes mistreated or misused?
5. What can you learn about God from this parable?
6. Discuss what God is expecting from his followers as they wait for the second coming of Christ.
7. Give some reasons why Jesus didn't provide more information about his ultimate return.
8. How has our waiting for God been inadequate at times?
9. What is the secret of being ready?
10. List some practical applications of "having your treasures in the right place."

ACTIVITIES

As a group: Reflect on/discuss how your experience of this book—including the parables and other Scripture, insights from the author, and your own reflections and discussions—have encouraged and challenged you.

At home: Create a list of changes you would like to make in your spiritual life that were inspired by your reading/ discussion of this book, reading your Bible, or talking with God in prayer. Lay out an action plan for making these changes in your life, and in prayer ask God to give you direction, encouragement, and resolve.

Prayer: *Dear God, thank you for your son, Jesus Christ, and for the stories and lessons he has shared with us. Thank you for opening our eyes to new truths through Jesus, and help us to apply them in our lives and for the benefit of others in our service to you. Help us seek to do your will each day, and to reflect to others your love for all of us. Amen.*